CHURCH SHIFT

THE GUIDE

First Edition
CHURCH*SHIFT* — THE GUIDE
ISBN *978-1-931682-27-5*

Published by Resolute Books
P. O. Box 93234
Southlake, TX 76092

www.ResoluteBooks.com

Printed in the United States of America

CHURCH SHIFT

THE GUIDE

by

Sunday Adelaja

WHAT PEOPLE ARE SAYING ABOUT

CHURCHSHIFT

God has raised up Sunday Adelaja to lead men and women to a deeper understanding of their spiritual destinies. Read this book, and let the journey begin.

~ Rear Admiral Barry Black (Ret.)
Chaplain, U.S. Senate

Nothing like the Embassy of God has ever been seen before in Ukraine.

~ British Broadcasting Corporation (BBC)

The Embassy of The Blessed Kingdom of God for All Nations church has ballooned from a ministry for society's troubled into this ex-Soviet republic's first true megachurch.

~ Associated Press (AP)

Pastor Sunday is a man with a mission.

~ Wall Street Journal

I have heard and read a great deal about Pastor Sunday and about the work he is doing. All those who do great things go through attacks such as Pastor Sunday has endured.

~ *Former U. S. President Bill Clinton*

Sunday Adelaja is a leading figure, not only in the Ukraine, but in the world. He has a spirit of faith driven by his compassion for people. The word he speaks is one of authority!

~ Billy Joe Daugherty
Founding Pastor, Victory Christian Center
Tulsa, OK

Some are called to churches. Some called to cities. Sunday Adelaja has a fresh word for the nations!

~ Kenneth C. Ulmer, D.Min., Ph.D.
Presiding Bishop, Macedonia International Bible Fellowship
Los Angeles, CA

I was gripped by Sunday Adelaja's brilliant grasp of the interrelationship between biblical truths and public policy.

~ Dr. Jim Garlow
Senior Pastor, Skyline Wesleyan Church
San Diego, CA

Thank you for your contribution to our common victory. Your conscious work is a considerable factor in that victory. It was you who protected democracy in Ukraine, standing for its high ideals and not considering your own interests. I am convinced that as long as there are people in Ukraine who have the same civil position, dignity and spirit as you have, everything will be alright in this country.

~ Victor Yushchenko
The President of Ukraine

Through Pastor Sunday's endeavours we have become bold and fearless people who are able to stand for truth, liberty and for God.

~ Leonid Chernovetskiy
Mayor of Kyiv, Ukraine

The most successful in contemporary European churches is the Ukraine-based ministry of Sunday Adelaja...

~ Philip Jenkins
Distinguished Professor of History and Religious studies, Pennsylvania State University, Missiologist, Author of *The Next Christendom: The Coming of Global Christianity*

Sunday Adelaja is an indisputable success in his family, in his church, in his nation.... This book will help you grow personally and spiritually. Read it and SUCCEED!

~ Peter Lowe
Founder and CEO, Get Motivated Seminars

I know of no Minister around the world that is more unique and influential than Bishop Sunday Adelaja. The supernatural principles of this book are radical, controversial and life changing. They will make ministers of the Gospel reconsider their place and calling in ministry. Our minds will be stretched and our concepts will be challenged, as they should be, for more effective 21st Century ministry.

~ Dr. Wendell Smith
Senior Pastor, The City Church
Seattle, WA

Strong Kingdom visionary leadership is required in order to fulfill the Great Commission in our lifetime. Pastor Sunday Adelaja presents a powerful pathway to empower both the pastor and the church for societal transformation.

~ Phil Pringle
Founder, Christian City Churches
Sydney, Australia

In order to reclaim America's communities, a dynamic leadership paradigm shift will need to take place in our local churches. Pastor Sunday Adelaja has provided a pathway for us to achieve success.

~ Alton Garrison
Assistant General Superintendent, Assemblies of God
Springfield, MO

Pastor Sunday Adelaja has been used by the Lord to transform his society for Christ. In CHURCH*SHIFT*, he teaches how one can learn how to take full responsibility and begin to climb the ladder of true greatness in life.

~ Pastor Stan Toler
Senior Pastor, Trinity Church of the Nazarene
Oklahoma City, OK

CHURCH*SHIFT* is a study in contemporary application of the relevant Kingdom Principles taught by Jesus Christ, and give evidence that the real mission, purpose and mandate of the church is not to abandon earth but to affect and infect it with the culture and nature of heaven.

~ Dr. Myles E. Munroe
Founder/President BFM International
International Third World Leaders Association (ITWLA)

In a meek yet bold way, Pastor Sunday shows the world how to make the Gospel socially relevant. His words will challenge you.

~ Bishop Dale C. Bronner, D. Min.
Founding Pastor, Word Of Faith Family Worship Cathedral
Atlanta, GA

Reading these pages, you will be inspired to live a greater life than you have ever dreamed possible.

~ James O. Davis
Co-Chair/Founder, Second Billion

CHURCH*SHIFT* will stretch your mind through God-given principles being applied in personal and powerful ways. You will understand your uniqueness in Christ and will have greater faith to experience supernatural results.

~ David Mohan
Founding Pastor, New Life Assembly
Chennai, India

Sunday has practically applied the principles of the Kingdom to his life, church, city, nation, and the world in every sphere of life and it is bringing transformation. The only hope of seeing transformation in our world is the living out of the principles he teaches from God's Word about the Kingdom.

~ Bob Roberts
Senior Pastor, NorthWood Church, Keller, TX
Author, Transformation and Glocalization

Pastor Sunday is a young old man: young because of his age of forty years old, old because at such a young age he has known what old men like me know and has been able to accomplish what many old men like me have not been able to do.

~ T. L. Osborn
International Evangelist
Tulsa, OK

God's mandate to us is nothing less than taking dominion of His entire creation here on earth. No one has put this mandate into practice more wisely and effectively than Sunday Adelaja.

~ C. Peter Wagner
Presiding Apostle, International Coalition of Apostles

Sunday Adelaja is one of those new breed of men who is influencing a nation, and modeling a new style of missions. He is a cross-cultural missionary who has made a new mold of what missions can do, to touch a nation. I consider Pastor Sunday a modern day hero of the Faith.

~ Pastor Robert Barriger
Founding Pastor, Camino de Vida
Lima, Peru

What a mark Pastor Sunday has made on Ukraine, Europe, and the world! I applaud his vision for ministry.

~ John Sorensen
Executive Vice President, Evangelism Explosion International

This book provides God's model for transformation and the mind-set of a Christ-centered revolution all from an incredible man who has led and experienced them both.

~ Dr. Ben Lerner
New York Times Best-Selling Author, U.S. Olympic Team Physician

This book will be a catalyst in leading a strategic church in today's world. I cannot wait to see this book read by thousands of pastors and church leaders like me who are hungry for a powerful and extraordinary move of God to impact our cities and nations.

~ David A. Sobrepeña
Founding Pastor, Word of Hope Church
Manila, Philippines

Sunday Adelaja is a man of great influence for the cause of Christ. Catch the largeness of his spirit, and find the greatness of God unfolding in your life.

~ Paul Louis Cole
President, Christian Men's Network

Sunday Adelaja's ministry inspires people all over the world. For those who live where Christians are persecuted, we are encouraged to see God quickly bring a nation from religious repression to freedom of religion and democracy. We are inspired to see God use a pastor to bring national transformation. Thank you, Sunday, for providing hope and for setting such a bold example.

~ Eddy Leo
Founding Pastor, Abbalove Ministries
Jakarta, Indonesia

If there is one book that can change your life, you're holding it in your hand. CHURCH*SHIFT* is one of the most important and timely messages that you will ever read. It's revolutionary!

~ Sam Hinn
Senior Pastor, The Gathering Place Worship Center
Sanford, FL

Kingdom leaders expand our spiritual horizons and cause us to see the world from God's perspective. CHURCH*SHIFT* challenges the reader to trust God for the resources required to bring societal transformation.

~ J. Don George
Senior Pastor, Calvary Church
Irving, TX

In today's fatherless world, where men abdicate their roles and shun responsibility, God must raise up fathers who will accept responsibility for families, communities, and nations. Sunday Adelaja, a fatherless child, has become a father to a nation.

~ J. Doug Stringer
Founder and President, Somebody Cares
Houston, TX

In CHURCH*SHIFT*, Sunday Adelaja articulates the greatest need Christians have today — for churches not just to be large, but to be large in influence. This book will help not only to build churches but to take nations.

~ Alexey Ledyaev
Senior Pastor, New Generation Churches
Riga, Latvia

The Embassy of God church is the biggest church in Ukraine and well-organized. Pastor Sunday is a unique man. This is a big church that keeps growing everyday.

~ Vasiliy Onopenko
Chairman of the Supreme Court of Ukraine

ABOUT THIS GUIDE

We are delighted that you hold this book in your hand today. It is the culmination of a 20-year pathway that led its author, Sunday Adelaja, to become an unlikely ambassador. Born in Nigeria, educated in the former USSR, and now pastoring in the nation of Ukraine, Pastor Sunday's message is for people who lead and attend church everywhere.

Our goal with this guide is to help churches all over America and the world to experience a *SHIFT* in the way they "do church." This will bring a *SHIFT* in how church members experience church, and a *SHIFT* in how the society views church and the Kingdom. This *SHIFT* will help you become more Kingdom-minded than ever! It is Pastor Sunday's express intention that the study of CHURCH*SHIFT* would equip and help the church in the following ways:

- Transform America and the Church worldwide by introducing a new way to do church
- Empower pastors to "pastor without tears"
- Avoid church splits and division
- Change every Christian's view of "Ministry"
- Inspire Christians to believe for supernatural outcomes
- Equip church members to impact the seven spheres of society
- Teach Kingdom values for societal transformation
- Activate the potential of the local church
- Change a nation by emerging from four church walls
- Provide the keys to achieve NATIONAL TRANSFORMATION!

How to use this guide to *SHIFT*

Pastor Sunday has poured over every word of this guide to ensure it teaches and empowers you to *SHIFT*. As people *SHIFT* their Christian focus, the world around them will take notice!

This book has THIRTEEN LESSONS. Each lesson has THREE PARTS:

1. *SHIFT* Challenge: These thought-provoking essays aimed at leaders, members or the whole church are unique to the guide, and not found in the CHURCH*SHIFT* book. Pastor Sunday wrote these lessons to help your mind fully comprehend the *SHIFT*. You may choose to include these to promote healthy discussion in your group study, or read them individually.
2. Part One: Interactive questions and activities based on the CHURCH*SHIFT* book.
3. Part Two: Thoughts to help you learn by example, summarize, reflect and act.

As you go through each lesson, there is ample space on each page to write your thoughts of what God is speaking to your heart.

The Seven Spheres of Society

Throughout our study, you will see Pastor Sunday refer to the seven spheres of society to which we carry our Kingdom lifestyle and principles. Here is a quick reference of the seven spheres:

1. Spiritual/Social
2. Government/Politics
3. Business/Economy
4. Education/Science
5. Media
6. Culture/Entertainment
7. Sports

You may find additional help and resources at www.churchshift.org

ENJOY the *SHIFT!* This guide may well be the most challenging exercise you ever attempt. It is certain to be the most satisfying and fulfilling!

SHIFT CHALLENGE 1

CHURCH*SHIFT*

SHIFTING YOUR MIND, *SHIFTING* THE CHURCH

What is "Ecclesia"?
Hebrews 13:1-12; John 17:15

At some time in our Christian lives, we will hear the word "ecclesia." Most of us leave the meaning to theologians to figure out. But we are going to start our study together with this word, because it is important to understand it in order to understand our need to *SHIFT*.

Many Christians define "ecclesia" as "separation from the world" or "called out from the world." Some expand this teaching and encourage Christians to run for shelter and hide from the world. Other churches simply use "ecclesia" as interchangeable with "the church." Both definitions can be correct, yet there is even greater application in the New Testament.

"Ecclesia" was used by the Apostle Paul specifically to describe the redeemed who are called out of the world system, away from their culture's values, so they can live by the higher Kingdom value system. "Ecclesia" was not intended to say that Christians are called out from the world in order to run and hide, but that we remain in the world yet are no longer ruled by its values and standards.

As "ecclesia," you and I are called to be separated from the world system and values but not from daily interaction with the world (John 4:4). We simply no longer embrace the values of the world. We don't love the values of the world. We love God Who is superior to the world He created for us (John 3:31).

Jesus brought balance and understanding for the health of His disciples before He left (John 17:15). He knew that totally separating ourselves from the world would mean:

1. Removing ourselves from those we are meant to save.
2. Hoarding and conserving the power and resources of God in the church.
3. Removing and keeping the light away from the darkness (Matthew 5:12-14).
4. Keeping the salt from the food.
5. Removing the mustard seed from the field, the yeast from the flour.
6. Stopping Kingdom values from permeating the earth.

7. Preventing Kingdom glory from invading the earth (Habakkuk 2:13-14; Isaiah 11:9; Genesis 2:15).

Jesus wants the Church to train and release Christians so that each of us will bring God's glory to earth. *"Go ye therefore..."* (Matthew 28:19-20). The Church is God's hope to restore the earth (Ephesians 3:8-10). The Church is the pillar of Kingdom truth (2 Timothy 3:15). The Church will eventually rule the earth (Isaiah 2:1-3; Revelation 5:10).

SHIFT YOUR THINKING:

1. Have you heard the word "ecclesia"? What definition have you previously learned?

2. How can shifting your mind-set about "ecclesia" shift your church or group?

3. As "ecclesia," you and I are called to be separated from the world system and values but not from daily interaction with the world (John 4:4). How can this be done practically?

Lesson One

Let the Revolution Begin

PART ONE

Read the book: Prologue & People Power

The church is ready for a *SHIFT* today. The world needs us to *SHIFT!* Areas of society that are longing for our Kingdom influence as believers are social, political, business, education, arts and entertainment, media and sports.

The revolution in Ukraine began in the prayer closet. It began when the church discovered how to *SHIFT* our mind-set as individuals and as a body of believers, empowering us to be used to change the mind-set of an entire country. It was a dramatic demonstration of God's intent for all believers to occupy society's spheres to transform entire nations.

Apply the principles, tools, and strategies in these pages to embrace your earthly assignment to occupy, establish the Kingdom of God in your everyday life, dethrone the kingdom of darkness, find your promised land of effectiveness where you live, work, and play, and impact the people, society, and nation where God has placed you. Transform your nation for Christ by taking simple steps daily to establish His rule and invite His glory. Be the head, not the tail. Pioneer social answers. Be a part of God's master plan to fulfill the Great Commission.

Get ready to *SHIFT*!

SHIFT STUDY: You Will Learn

- The Church fulfills its mandate when it changes society, not when it is confined to its sanctuary and Sunday school classrooms.
- This isolation of the Church from the world has led to ineffectiveness and failure to carry out the Great Commission.
- The Great Commission mandate is to go out and disciple nations.
- Ministry is what you do to bring your life and your sphere of influence under Kingdom rule.
- We are not called to huddle inside the church sanctuary but to restore the Kingdom of God to the world.
- God holds the Church responsible for societies.
- The Church is to be the training ground for people who will impact the society around them.

SHIFT SCRIPTURES:

Prayer Warriors

"And I set my face unto the Lord God, to seek by prayer and supplications, with fasting, and sackcloth, and ashes" Daniel 9:3.

"And she was a widow of about fourscore and four years, which departed not from the temple, but served God with fastings and prayers night and day" Luke 2:37.

"But we will give ourselves continually to prayer, and to the ministry of the word" Acts 6:4.

"Confess your faults one to another, and pray one for another, that ye may be healed. The effectual fervent prayer of a righteous man availeth much" James 5:16.

Personal Prayer

"Rejoicing in hope; patient in tribulation; continuing instant in prayer" Romans 12:12.

"Praying always with all prayer and supplication in the Spirit, and watching thereunto with all perseverance and supplication for all saints" Ephesians 6:18.

"Be careful for nothing; but in every thing by prayer and supplication with thanksgiving let your requests be made known unto God" Philippians 4:6.

A. *SHIFT* Your Life

1. Does anything concern you in your own community, city or nation?

2. What concerns you *most?*

3. What would a community look like that was being impacted and overtaken by the churches in it?

   Who would be featured in news media reports?

   How would schools be operated?

   What would the crime rate be?

   Where would community and church monies be spent?

   When would a child begin learning about Jesus?

4. What gifts and abilities do you have to offer your community?

B. Laying a Foundation

The foundation of prayer must be laid to be sure we are in tune with God. Through prayer, we receive the strength and wisdom needed for the task ahead.

Read the following verses of Scripture here and in your favorite Bible translation:

"For other foundation can no man lay than that is laid, which is Jesus Christ" 1 Corinthians 3:11.

"Laying up in store for themselves a good foundation against the time to come, that they may lay hold on eternal life" 1 Timothy 6:19.

1. Do you believe that every Christian should be a "prayer warrior"?

   Why?

   Why do we need to be fervent in prayer?

2. How does your experience in prayer compare to "prayer warriors" you know?

3. What is Pastor Sunday's point about the prayer time required for him and his church to hear and receive God's instructions?

4. Describe what you could do in your prayer closet and what you would expect to achieve.

"I exhort therefore, that, first of all, supplications, prayers, intercessions, and giving of thanks, be made for all men" 1 Timothy 2:1.

Corporate Prayer

"Even them will I bring to my holy mountain, and make them joyful in my house of prayer: their burnt offerings and their sacrifices shall be accepted upon mine altar; for mine house shall be called an house of prayer for all people" Isaiah 56:7.

"Men ought always to pray, and not to faint" Luke 18:1.

"These all continued with one accord in prayer and supplication, with the women, and Mary the mother of Jesus, and with his brethren" Acts 1:14.

"Peter therefore was kept in prison: but prayer was made without ceasing of the church unto God for him" Acts 12:5.

Prayer Results

"And when they had prayed ... they spake the word of God with boldness" Acts 4:31.

"If my people, which are called by my name, shall humble themselves, and pray, and seek my face, and turn from their wicked ways; then will I hear from heaven, and will forgive their sin, and will heal their land" 2 Chronicles 7:14.

"Hear me when I call, O God of my righteousness: thou hast enlarged me when I was in distress; have mercy upon me, and hear my prayer" Psalm 4:1.

"My voice shalt thou hear in the morning, O LORD; in the morning will I direct my prayer unto thee, and will look up" Psalm 5:3.

"Hear my prayer, O LORD, give ear to my supplications: in thy faithfulness answer me, and in thy righteousness" Psalm 143:1.

"For the eyes of the Lord are over the righteous, and his ears are open unto their prayers: but the face of the Lord is against them that do evil" 1 Peter 3:12.

God's Kingdom

"Therefore do not be like them. For your Father knows the things you have need of before you ask Him. In this manner, therefore, pray: Our Father in heaven, Hallowed be Your name. Your kingdom come. Your will be done On earth as it is in heaven" Matthew 6:8-10 NKJV.

"He left Judea and departed again to Galilee. But He needed to go through Samaria...Jesus answered and said to her, 'Whoever drinks of this water will thirst again, but whoever drinks of the water that I shall give him will never thirst. But the water that I shall give him will become in him a fountain of water springing up into everlasting life.' The woman said

What changes could you make to your schedule to achieve this?

C. The Kingdom of God

1. Fill in: *(page 5)*

   But God opened my eyes to see that to complete

   the Great Commission, we must have

   ________________ upon ________________,

   not just ______________ in ______________.

   Transforming ____________ requires bold steps.

2. Explain in your own words what this statement means: "The Great Commission is not primarily concerned with building churches but with building the Kingdom of God in every sphere of society." *(pages 6-8)*

3. What is a major difference between "church" and the "Kingdom of God"? *(page 10)*

D. Preparation for the Race

To occupy your "Promised Land," God will often call you to do things you have never done before. He asked Sunday's church to protest openly yet peacefully against their government. This required them to overcome a mind-set of oppression, complacency, and fear. They had to question authority, show leadership with accountability, mobilize themselves, and dare to step out of line. They all knew that the last people who protested had been shot!

When Pastor Sunday asked them to take this bold action, many in his church rejected it as suicidal, unbiblical. Leaders resigned. People left the church. Sunday instructed the people to seek God about His Word to them to influence their nation by getting outside the four walls of their church.

1. If you were in Pastor Sunday's church, would you have followed him in this first march? Would you have watched from the sidelines and waited to see what happened? What would make the difference for you?

to Him, 'Sir, give me this water, that I may not thirst, nor come here to draw'" John 4:2-4, 13-15 NKJV.

God's Will

"For I have come down from heaven, not to do My own will, but the will of Him who sent Me" John 6:38 NKJV.

"I delight to do Your will, O my God, And Your law is within my heart" Psalm 40:8 NKJV.

"Again, a second time, He went away and prayed, saying, 'O My Father, if this cup cannot pass away from Me unless I drink it, Your will be done'" Matthew 26:42 NKJV.

"Teach me to do Your will, For You are my God; Your Spirit is good. Lead me in the land of uprightness" Psalm 143:10 NKJV.

"Now this is the confidence that we have in Him, that if we ask anything according to His will, He hears us. And if we know that He hears us, whatever we ask, we know that we have the petitions that we have asked of Him" I John 5:14-15 NKJV.

"But He answered and said to the one who told Him, 'Who is My mother and who are My brothers?' And He stretched out His hand toward His disciples and said, 'Here are My mother and My brothers! For whoever does the will of My Father in heaven is My brother and sister and mother'" Matthew 12:46-50 NKJV.

World-Changers

"Therefore You delivered them into the hand of their enemies, Who oppressed them; And in the time of their trouble, When they cried to You, You heard from heaven; And according to Your abundant mercies You gave them deliverers who saved them From the hand of their enemies" Nehemiah 9:27 NKVJ.

"When the children of Israel cried out to the LORD, the LORD raised up a deliverer for the children of Israel, who delivered them." Judges 3:9-11 NKJV.

"The LORD said to my Lord, 'Sit at My right hand, Till I make Your enemies Your footstool.' The LORD shall send the rod of Your strength out of Zion. Rule in the midst of Your enemies! Your people shall be volunteers In the day of Your power; In the beauties of holiness, from the womb of the morning, You have the dew of Your youth" Psalm 110:1-3 NKJV.

2. The Church is the equipping place for world changers. Name some Christian people who changed the world.

3. God holds believers responsible for their nation. God needs believers to take a strong stand for righteousness. In what areas of your life do you need to risk making a tough decision, similar to taking the risk of marching? *(page 9)*

PART TWO

SHIFT STUDY:

Historical Perspective: Presbyterian Church

More than half of the soldiers and officers in America's Revolutionary army were Presbyterians; all but one of the colonels were Presbyterian elders. In fact, the War for Independence was referred to in Britain as the "Presbyterian rebellion."

"The Revolution of 1776, so far as it was affected by religion, was a Presbyterian measure," wrote American historian George Bancroft.

One ardent colonial supporter wrote to King George III the following words: "I fix all of the blame for these extraordinary proceedings upon the Presbyterians. They have been the chief and principal instruments in all these flaming measures."

When Independence was won and the battlefield smoke cleared, the government that took shape also was attributed to the Church. The form of government that existed in the Presbyterian Church was the only "republic" existing on the North American continent for 75 years before 1776. This form of Church government is the one which the American government, to a great extent, simply mirrored.[1]

SHIFT PRAYER:

Father, I thank You that I am Your image, Your representative on the earth to cause Your will to be done on earth as it is in heaven. I therefore commit myself to seek Your face, obey, and act as You will lead me until Your purpose comes to pass in my country, city, and areas of influence. Thank You, Lord, for hearing and enabling me. In Jesus' name, Amen.

SHIFT MEDITATION:

The Church of the living God, [is] the pillar and foundation of the truth 1 Timothy 3:15 NIV.

The Bible is the rock on which our republic rests.
~ Andrew Jackson

[1]Excerpted from Dr. D. James Kennedy, Adapted from *"The Man Who Founded America"*; www.coralridge.org

"And to make all see what is the fellowship of the mystery, which from the beginning of the ages has been hidden in God who created all things through Jesus Christ; to the intent that now the manifold wisdom of God might be made known by the church to the principalities and powers in the heavenly places" Ephesians 3:9-10 NKJV.

"For the Son of Man has come to seek and to save that which was lost" Luke 19:10 NKJV.

SHIFT CHALLENGE 2

LEADER*SHIFT*

SHIFTING THE LEADERS, *SHIFTING* THE CHURCH

A Counterfeit Ministry?
Mark 12:37; Matthew 25; Matthew 9:34; Matthew 4:23-25

Today, the Gospel message is preached more and with greater understanding and revelation than ever before in history. As glorious and wonderful as the pulpit is these days, it is difficult not to notice a common misunderstanding of pulpit ministry. To a degree, the pulpit can become a "counterfeit ministry."

Well-meaning church members can believe the pulpit is the *only* ministry in the church, and bring their unsaved friends and colleagues to the pastor for salvation, counsel and every kind of aid and assistance. Well-meaning ministers may assume the pulpit is "their ministry." Both parties erroneously see the pulpit as the place where "ministry" mostly occurs. This is an easy, conventional, sentimental, and historical trap, into which I naturally fell in my early years as a pastor.

My thinking as a young pastor centered on getting "anointed" or getting a "Big Revelation" so that we could have a good church service. I thought that if I prepared and performed well, then people would come to church in droves, and I'd be a "Big Success." Back then, my weekly focus was to fast and pray to get an "anointing," and study to receive a "Big Revelation." As it turned out, the ministry God built in Ukraine was not based on my oratory skills each week. Instead, our church grew when I focused on leading people out into the world with Kingdom values.

The problem with a "pulpit-only" view of ministry is that members can become lethargic and dependent on pastors for their faith and needs. Pastors can become self-focused and performance-oriented, almost like actors, rather than manifesting and revealing God's power through our lifestyle every day. The Good Samaritan story teaches us that the pulpit and the stage are not always the expression of Kingdom ministry (Luke 10:30-37). The priest and Levite passed by the need. The Samaritan understood that "ministry" is to whomever is needy and whenever or wherever a need presents itself.

Good Samaritan pastors do not focus just on pulpit ministry. Good Samaritan members do not wait for the pastor to do all the ministry. *True ministry is in touching lives with God's love and touching God with men's needs.*

Jesus showed us that ministry is about our daily lifestyle and revealing God to our society and nation through our lives (Matthew 7:21-24; 25:34; Mark 12:37). A community leader, business person, entertainer or politician may faithfully attend church services and even invite others, yet not release God in their sphere of influence all week long. God is interested in our daily demonstration of Kingdom values (Matthew 9:34-35; Matthew 4:23-24). Preaching and the pulpit are *tools* to manifest the Kingdom. They are not "the ministry." At times pastors have to leave the pulpit to go to people, and members have to relieve the pastor of the total responsibility for ministering to the entire community.

Ministry is not eloquence and oratory. It is changing lives through Kingdom values. Ministry is every Christian's privilege and responsibility—to touch lives with God's love and to touch God with men's needs.

SHIFT YOUR THINKING:

1. What do you think of when you think of "ministry"?

2. What are the dangers, for both pastors and members, of focusing only on the pulpit as "ministry"?

3. What could you do today to shift your thinking about ministry? In what way could you minister all week long?

Lesson Two

God Did Not Create a Passive Church

PART ONE

Read the book: The Kingdom-Minded Church

The decision to stand up to our government became a watershed moment for us and for the entire nation of Ukraine. We had very good reason to believe our lives were in danger if we went to the streets in protest, but the destiny of our land was in the hands of the Church and her willingness to declare the Kingdom God in our society.

God wants the Church to become the standard-bearer of order and righteousness and to use faith to subdue and change nations. The reward for seeking God is influence over a sphere of society so people can be rescued from the horrors of sin and evil. We had to see ourselves as instruments in God's hand, to shift our thinking from hiding in church to ruling our Promised Land for the glory of God. We didn't have the moral right to be indifferent. We marched on city hall.

God was about to put us on the vanguard of a much bigger movement than we had bargained for!

SHIFT STUDY: You Will Learn

- God eagerly awaits the redemption of the nations.
- God wants preeminence in all things in every nation.
- Until the children of the almighty God act like His representatives on the earth, nothing will change in our countries. The destiny of our countries is in the hands of the Church and her willingness to declare the position of God in the society.
- The real focus of every Christian's life and of all our church activities is promoting the kingdom of God in every sphere of our nations.
- If the Church doesn't start fighting corruption, it will keep flourishing in the country.
- A church that is not focused on discipling nations exchanges its big ambitions for small ones without even realizing it.
- If you want to use your faith to get a new car or more church members, fine. But I'm using my faith to subdue and change a nation.

SHIFT SCRIPTURES:

God is After Nations

"For He has not put the world to come...in subjection to angels. But one testified in a certain place, saying: 'What is man that You are mindful of him, Or the son of man that You take care of him? You have made him a little lower than the angels; You have crowned him with glory and honor, And set him over the works of Your hands. You have put all things in subjection under his feet.' For in that He put all in subjection under him, He left nothing that is not put under him. But now we do not yet see all things put under him" Hebrews 2:5-8 NKJV.

"The heaven, even the heavens, are the LORD's; But the earth He has given to the children of men" Psalm 115:16 NKJV.

"Thus says the LORD: 'In an acceptable time I have heard You, And in the day of salvation I have helped You; I will preserve You and give You As a covenant to the people, To restore the earth, To cause them to inherit the desolate heritages'" Isaiah 49:8 NKJV.

A. God Is After Nations

Nations are as tangible and precious to God as individuals are.

1. How do you know God's concern is not limited to individuals? *(page 17)*

2. Why does God teach us to obey, respect, and submit to the authority of man's governments? *(page 18)*

3. What do you believe your own individual responsibility is to government on a

   - family level?
   - church level?
   - government level?
   - global level?

4. How can parents encourage a "national focus" in the home? How about a "global focus"?

B. Man Is to Spread the Kingdom of God

1. Fill in: *(page 20)*

God gave us this corner of the universe to __________, just as He is ________________ over the universe. Adam was created in the ___________________ and after the likeness of God to ______________________ the earth. He fellowshipped and communed with God; he dressed and ______________________ the Garden of Eden. The glory of the Kingdom was present in the Garden of Eden, and men were to _____________ it.

Starting with Adam, is it typical for God's people to take care of the world God created for us?

Do most Christians think in terms of discipling the nations?

Authorities

"But sanctify the Lord God in your hearts: and be ready always to give an answer to every man that asketh you a reason of the hope that is in you with meekness and fear" 1 Peter 3:15.

"Let every soul be subject unto the higher powers. For there is no power but of God: the powers that be are ordained of God. Whosoever therefore resisteth the power, resisteth the ordinance of God: and they that resist shall receive to themselves damnation. For rulers are not a terror to good works, but to the evil. Wilt thou then not be afraid of the power? do that which is good, and thou shalt have praise of the same: For he is the minister of God to thee for good. But if thou do that which is evil, be afraid; for he beareth not the sword in vain: for he is the minister of God, a revenger to execute wrath upon him that doeth evil. Wherefore ye must needs be subject, not only for wrath, but also for conscience sake." Romans 13:1-5

"Without wise leadership, a nation is in trouble" Proverbs 11:14 TLB.

"When there is moral rot within a nation, its government topples easily; but with honest, sensible leaders there is stability" Proverbs 28:2 TLB.

"With good men in authority, the people rejoice; but with the wicked in power, they groan" Proverbs 29:2 TLB.

Our Responsibility

"Then God said, 'Let Us make man in Our image, according to Our likeness; let them have dominion over the fish of the sea, over the birds of the air, and over the cattle, over all the earth and over every creeping thing that creeps on the earth.' So God created man in His own image; in the image of God He created him; male and female He created them. Then God blessed them, and God said to them, 'Be fruitful and multiply; fill the earth and subdue it; have dominion over the fish of the sea, over the birds of the air, and over every living thing that moves on the earth'" Genesis 1:26-28 NKJV.

"For the earnest expectation of the creation eagerly waits for the revealing of the sons of God. For the creation was subjected to futility, not willingly, but because of Him who subjected it in hope; because the creation itself also will be delivered from the bondage of corruption into the glorious liberty of the children of God. For we know that

Is it possible in our present day and time for Christians to exercise a "Kingdom" purpose in society?

2. Read the following verses of Scripture here and in your favorite Bible translation:

   "...Occupy till I come" Luke 19:13.

   "...Jesus came...preaching the gospel of the kingdom of God, and saying, The time is fulfilled, and the kingdom of God is at hand: repent ye, and believe the gospel" Mark 1:15.

   "...No doubt the kingdom of God is come upon you" Luke 11:20.

   How do these influence your thoughts concerning the Kingdom?

3. "The real focus of every Christian's life, and of all our church activities, is promoting the Kingdom of God in every sphere of our nations." *(page 20)*

   Do you believe that spreading the Kingdom of God is your job? Explain.

   How can the church/believers fight corruption? Give practical examples.

C. God Expects Us to Move in Authority and Power

1. Meditate or discuss what these Scripture verses mean:

   "And hast made us unto our God kings and priests: and we shall reign on the earth" Revelation 5:10.

   "But you are a chosen people, a royal priesthood, a holy nation, a people belonging to God, that you may declare the praises of him who called you out of darkness into his wonderful light" 1 Peter 2:9.

2. "A church not focused on discipling nations exchanges big ambitions for small ones." *(page 23-24)*

   Estimate the "ambition size" of your church with reasons supporting your assessment.

   What is the difference between a large church and a church with large impact?

the whole creation groans and labors with birth pangs together until now" Romans 8:19-22 NKJV.

"Behold, I will make you small among the nations; You shall be greatly despised" Obadiah 2 NKJV.

"And He Himself gave some to be apostles, some prophets, some evangelists, and some pastors and teachers, for the equipping of the saints for the work of ministry, for the edifying of the body of Christ, till we all come to the unity of the faith and of the knowledge of the Son of God, to a perfect man, to the measure of the stature of the fullness of Christ" Ephesians 4:11-13 NKJV.

"And Jesus came and spoke to them, saying, 'All authority has been given to Me in heaven and on earth. Go therefore and make disciples of all the nations, baptizing them in the name of the Father and of the Son and of the Holy Spirit, teaching them to observe all things that I have commanded you; and lo, I am with you always, even to the end of the age.' Amen" Matthew 28:18-20 NKJV.

"And have made us kings and priests to our God; And we shall reign on the earth" Revelation 5:10 NKJV.

Our Authority and Power

"The wicked flee when no man pursueth; but the righteous are bold as a lion" Proverbs 28:1.

"So that we may boldly say, The Lord is my helper, and I will not fear what man shall do unto me" Hebrews 13:6.

"But as many as received him, to them gave he power to become the sons of God, even to them that believe on his name" John 1:12.

"Verily, verily, I say unto you, He that believeth on me, the works that I do shall he do also; and greater works than these shall he do; because I go unto my Father" John 14:12.

"For I am not ashamed of the gospel of Christ: for it is the power of God unto salvation to every one that believeth; to the Jew first, and also to the Greek. For therein is the righteousness of God revealed from faith to faith: as it is written, The just shall live by faith" Romans 1:16-17.

"And he that overcometh, and keepeth my works unto the end, to him will I give power over the nations: And he shall rule them with a rod of iron; as the vessels of a potter shall they be broken to shivers: even as I received of my Father" Revelation 2:26-27.

Taking Action

"For unto us a child is born, unto us a son is given: and the government shall be upon his shoulder: and his name shall be called Wonderful, Counsellor, The mighty God, The everlasting Father, The Prince of Peace. Of the increase of his

Have you been satisfied with only "tools" of faith, blessing or prosperity? How can you lift your faith from small satisfactions to great ambitions? *(page 23)*

D. The Time is NOW!

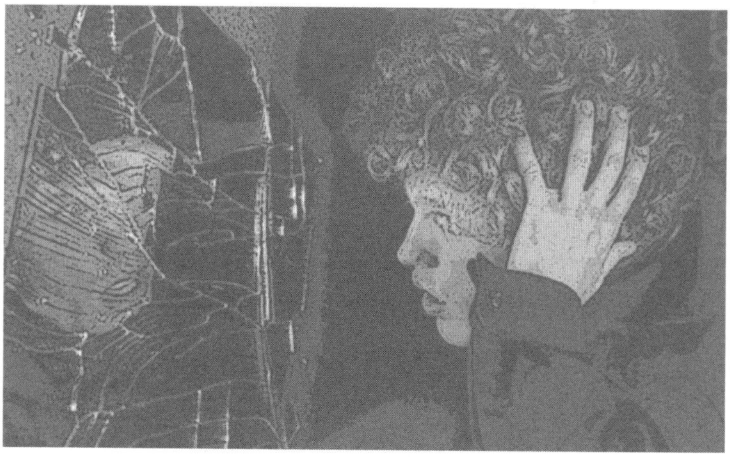

"Did the only begotten Son of God humble Himself and come here to be violently and brutally murdered, hung on a cross, despised and mocked, then come back from the dead and preach and teach for forty days just so we could be prosperous and have emotion-stirring praise and worship times and pass our colorful leaflets and set up clever websites all while people around us are depressed and committing suicide, spreading AIDS, dying of hunger, wrecking the planet, and much more?" *(page 24)*

It is time:
- to remember the Cross and the big ambitions Christ has for this planet
- to rule our Promised Land for the glory of God
- to ask, knock, and seek results
- to stop thinking of ourselves on the bottom rung of the social ladder
- to stop lying low

God is waiting for us to take action! We don't have the moral right to be indifferent. Read the following aloud:

- I am an instrument in God's hand. I hold and help determine the destiny of my family, friends, co-workers, and nation.
- I am not small or insignificant. I am God's messenger.
- I walk in power, exercising my gifts and talents. When I give up small satisfactions, I accept ambitions much larger than I ever dreamed!

Write two more proclamations for yourself:

1. ____________________________________

2. ____________________________________

Make a copy of these proclamations for your mirror, desk, computer, refrigerator, dashboard, backpack, PDA, or iPod.

"And thou shalt bind them for a sign upon thine hand, and they shall be as frontlets between thine eyes. And thou shalt write them upon the posts of thy house, and on thy gates" Deuteronomy 6:8-9.

government and peace there shall be no end, upon the throne of David, and upon his kingdom, to order it, and to establish it with judgment and with justice from henceforth even for ever. The zeal of the LORD of hosts will perform this" Isaiah 9:6-7.

"And this gospel of the kingdom shall be preached in all the world for a witness unto all nations; and then shall the end come" Matthew 24:14.

"Go ye into all the world, and preach the gospel to every creature" Mark 16:15.

Kingdom of God

"...For the earth shall be full of the knowledge of the LORD, as the waters cover the sea" Isaiah 11:9.

"And the glory of the LORD shall be revealed, and all flesh shall see it together: for the mouth of the LORD hath spoken it" Isaiah 40:5.

"And in the days of these kings shall the God of heaven set up a kingdom, which shall never be destroyed: and the kingdom shall not be left to other people, but it shall break in pieces and consume all these kingdoms, and it shall stand for ever" Daniel 2:44.

"For the earth shall be filled with the knowledge of the glory of the LORD, as the waters cover the sea" Habakuk 2:14.

PART TWO

SHIFT STUDY:

Historical Perspective: Martin Luther

Martin Luther, a German theologian, started the Protestant Reformation when he stated openly his observations of Scripture. Luther's theology challenged the authority of the Pope by emphasizing the Bible as the sole source of religious authority. According to Luther, salvation was attainable individually by faith in Jesus Christ, without the intercession of a priest.

At the time, the Holy Roman Empire sold indulgences that promised relief from sin and assurance of heaven. When a priest arrived in Luther's hometown of Wittenberg selling indulgences, Luther wrote a letter to the Archbishop of Mainz. He nailed the 95 theses of this letter to the door of the Wittenberg church. When he was declared a heretic, Luther stood his ground stating, "It is neither safe nor right to go against conscience. God help me."

Within ten years, Luther's Protestant movement spread beyond Germany. He translated the Bible into common vernacular, which had further impact on the culture and government. His hymns inspired what is now congregational singing. His marriage late in life opened the door for marriage among clergy. Martin Luther's ideas put into action changed the course of Western civilization.[1]

God's Word

"So shall I have wherewith to answer him that reproacheth me: for I trust in thy word. And take not the word of truth utterly out of my mouth; for I have hoped in thy judgments. So shall I keep thy law continually for ever and ever. And I will walk at liberty: for I seek thy precepts. I will speak of thy testimonies also before kings, and will not be ashamed" Psalm 119:42-46.

"Is not my word like as a fire? Saith the Lord; and like a hammer that breaketh the rock in pieces?" Jeremiah 23:29.

"For no word from God shall be void of power" Luke 1:37.

"And fear not them which kill the body, but are not able to kill the soul: but rather fear him which is able to destroy both soul and body in hell. Whosoever therefore shall confess me before men, him will I confess also before my Father which is in heaven" Matthew 10:28, 32, 33.

"And they overcame him (the devil) by the blood of the Lamb, and by the word of their testimony; and they loved not their lives unto the death" Revelation 12:11.

SHIFT PRAYER:

Heavenly Father, I ask You to please deliver me from domestic, self-focused lifestyle and goals. Please, Lord, expand my vision, my territory, and my ambition. Cause my ambition and passion to be more about Your concerns, ambition, and vision. Help me, Lord, to see like You, dream like You, and act like You. In Jesus' name, Amen.

SHIFT MEDITATION:

"Thus says the LORD: 'In an acceptable time I have heard You, And in the day of salvation I have helped You; I will preserve You and give You as a covenant to the people, To restore the earth, To cause them to inherit the desolate heritages'" Isaiah 49:8 NKJV.

"Where there is no vision [no redemptive revelation of God], the people perish; but he who keeps the law [of God, which includes that of man]—blessed (happy, fortunate, and enviable) is he" Proverbs 29:18 AMP.

REPEAT: "I am called and saved to restore the earth back to God, using my God-given gifts, abilities, and talents."

If he have faith, the believer cannot be restrained.
He betrays himself. He breaks out.
He confesses and teaches this gospel to the people at the risk of life itself.
~ Martin Luther

[1]Adapted from writings at www.fsmitha.com and www.wikipedia.org

SHIFT CHALLENGE 3

CHURCH*SHIFT*

SHIFTING THE CHURCH

Egocentric Enterprises
Colossians 3:1-3

"Thy Kingdom come, thy will be done on earth, as it is in heaven," is our prayer. God's dream and passion are for the Church to meet *God's* need, which is to make the kingdom of the world be subject to the Kingdom of our God (Luke 4:43). We are called to live for the One Who died for us (Galatians 2:20-22). He won us at a price, that we should live only for Him and not for ourselves (1 Peter 1:18-19).

With the advent of technology, the entire world has been able to watch huge scandals all over the globe. Egocentrism is generally at the root of these business, political and even church scandals. Egocentrism thrives in a culture of self-gratification. When leadership in a church, business, sports team or any other enterprise uses its members or partners as a means to meet personal needs, the whole organization can be corrupted. If leadership gets it wrong, then the whole organization can be led astray.

In egocentric businesses, leaders manipulate employees whom they view as a means to serve their own interests. Egocentric leaders breed a culture of self-gratification instead of self-sacrifice (Philippians 2:1-9; Matthew 6:22-23). In egocentric enterprises, people focus less on blessing others or even serving the company and more on being personally blessed. Employees begin to strive to gain power and influence through any available means.

Even churches can be egocentric. In an egocentric church, members see worship services as a place to have their needs met. Church then becomes a place to get a feel-good, "ear-tickling" message that "feeds the flesh" instead of "seeking the Kingdom" (Matthew 6:33). In a recent Top-100 list of Christian books in America, eleven centered on God. The remaining eighty-nine centered on self. Egocentric Christians desire "self-exploration" and seek "self-revelation" instead of exploring Scriptures and asking God to reveal Himself to us.

God formed the Church for Himself to teach us how to function here on the earth and how to take His Kingdom into the whole earth (1 Timothy 3:15). If the Church mimics the values of greed and ego from the earth, the Church and the entire earth will suffer. We are to spread the values of the Kingdom, including love and self-sacrifice. (Matthew 28:18-20; Romans 12:1, 2). Our goal in life is not seek to be blessed and have our wants and needs provided, but to be like Jesus and enforce His Kingdom principles on earth.

SHIFT YOUR THINKING:

1. What is your definition of "seeking the Kingdom"? In what way can a church foster that desire in its members' lives?

2. Based on what you've read above what would be the purpose of preaching, going to church, a job, salary? Is it for self-gratification or equipping for Kingdom service?

3. What can you do starting today to make yourself less egocentric?

Lesson Three

How Do I Get Started?

PART ONE

Read the book: Finding Your Promised Land

"How do I get started? What is my part?"

Go to God to discover your Promised Land—your area of gifting where you are naturally graceful and fruitful—where your love and pain intersect—where you feel an almost supernatural hunger to intervene and improve a situation. Your place of calling becomes your place of manifesting Christ as a servant.

Grow. Change. Train. Obey God. Be faithful. Wait. Prepare. Know your purpose. Pray. Explore. Investigate. Cultivate professionalism, service, and excellence.

Because knowledge focuses effort, expand outside of church programs and activities. Pursue further education in order to combine professional knowledge with knowledge of kingdom principles.

SHIFT from the four walls of your church to subduing every sphere of your life with God and kingdom principles.

A. Discover Your Promised Land

1. Define "Promised Land." *(pages 30-33)*

SHIFT STUDY:
You Will Learn

- Your promised land will always involve meeting other people's needs.
- When you confine true ministry to the fivefold ministries, you make ninety-five percent of the Church irrelevant.
- Don't confuse the chore you perform in God's house with the promised land He gives you outside His house.
- Your place of calling becomes your place of manifesting Christ as a servant.
- The best way to explore your promised land is through education.
- Knowledge must lead to righteousness.
- Nobody can go further than their knowledge.

SHIFT SCRIPTURES:

Your Promised Land

"Then it will be righteousness for us, if we are careful to observe all these commandments before the LORD our God, as He has commanded us" Deuteronomy 6:25 NKJV.

"And one cried to another and said: 'Holy, holy, holy is the LORD of hosts; The whole earth is full of His glory!'" Isaiah 6:3 NKJV.

"So I sought for a man among them who would make a wall, and stand in the gap before Me on behalf of the land, that I should not destroy it; but I found no one" Ezekiel 22:30 NKJV.

"So I have come down to deliver them out of the hand of the Egyptians, and to bring them up from that land to a good and large land, to a land flowing with milk and honey, to the place of the Canaanites and the Hittites and the Amorites and the Perizzites and the Hivites and the Jebusites" Exodus 3:8 NKJV.

"A land of wheat and barley, of vines and fig trees and pomegranates, a land of olive oil and honey; a land in which you will eat bread without scarcity, in which you will lack nothing; a land whose stones are iron and out of whose hills you can dig copper. When you have eaten and are full, then you shall bless the

2. Why is discovering your personal Promised Land of primary importance?

3. How does a Promised Land relate to evangelism? *(page 33)*

B. Break Free into Your Ministry

Read: *"But unto every one of us is given grace according to the measure of the gift of Christ. Wherefore he saith, When he ascended up on high, he led captivity captive, and gave gifts unto men...And he gave some, apostles; and some, prophets; and some, evangelists; and some, pastors and teachers; For the perfecting of the saints, for the work of the ministry, for the edifying of the body of Christ: Till we all come in the unity of the faith, and of the knowledge of the Son of God, unto a perfect man, unto the measure of the stature of the fulness of Christ"* Ephesians 4:11-13.

1. After reading this passage, explain the statement that "limiting ministry to the pulpit or to the fivefold ministries makes ninety-five percent of the Church irrelevant." *(page 33)*

2. Pulpit ministries are to:
   - help people discover and be effective in their own sphere of influence.
   - empower people with kingdom principles.
   - release people in confidence and strength.

Are pulpit ministries helping you with these elements?

3. Fill in: *(page 33)*

Your promised land is almost certainly

______________ a ministry you feel you

should ______________ but an actual place of

____________________ in society that you can

take back by the grace of God. *(page 34)*

Don't confuse the ____________________ you

perform in God's house for the ______________

______________ He gives you outside His house.

What chore are you doing in the Lord's house? *(page 34)*

What area could you "occupy" as part of your Promised Land outside the church?

LORD your God for the good land which He has given you. 'Beware that you do not forget the LORD your God by not keeping His commandments, His judgments, and His statutes which I command you today Deuteronomy 8:8-12 NKJV.

"And that you may prolong your days in the land which the LORD swore to give your fathers, to them and their descendants, 'a land flowing with milk and honey.' For the land which you go to possess is not like the land of Egypt from which you have come, where you sowed your seed and watered it by foot, as a vegetable garden; but the land which you cross over to possess is a land of hills and valleys, which drinks water from the rain of heaven, a land for which the LORD your God cares; the eyes of the LORD your God are always on it, from the beginning of the year to the very end of the year" Deuteronomy 11:9-12 NKJV.

"After the death of Moses the servant of the LORD, it came to pass that the LORD spoke to Joshua the son of Nun, Moses' assistant, saying: "Moses My servant is dead. Now therefore, arise, go over this Jordan, you and all this people, to the land which I am giving to them—the children of Israel. Every place that the sole of your foot will tread upon I have given you, as I said to Moses. From the wilderness

and this Lebanon as far as the great river, the River Euphrates, all the land of the Hittites, and to the Great Sea toward the going down of the sun, shall be your territory. No man shall be able to stand before you all the days of your life; as I was with Moses, so I will be with you. I will not leave you nor forsake you. Be strong and of good courage, for to this people you shall divide as an inheritance the land which I swore to their fathers to give them" Joshua 1:1-6 NKJV.

Finding Your Promised Land

"And He will set the sheep on His right hand, but the goats on the left. Then the King will say to those on His right hand, 'Come, you blessed of My Father, inherit the kingdom prepared for you from the foundation of the world: for I was hungry and you gave Me food; I was thirsty and you gave Me drink; I was a stranger and you took Me in; I was naked and you clothed Me; I was sick and you visited Me; I was in prison and you came to Me'" Matthew 25:33-36 NKJV.

"And if you have not been faithful in what is another man's, who will give you what is your own?... And He said to them, 'You are those who justify yourselves before men, but God knows your hearts. For what is highly esteemed among men is an abomina-

"Your place of calling becomes your place of manifesting Christ as a servant." Explain what this means to you and how it affects your actions. *(page 36)*

4. Re-read this statement: *(pages 36-37)*

   "If you have not found your own Promised Land, or if you are still in training, don't stand idly by, but help others find their Promised Lands. Our goal in subduing our own Promised Land is not about self-fulfillment or self-advancement. Nobody can excuse themselves from labor simply because they do not know where their Promised Land is. Ours is a common goal, not a one-man show."

   Who can you help in their Promised Land right now?

   How do you think this could help you find your own Promised Land?

   How do you discover your own Promised Land?

   How do you start out in your Promised Land?

C. Explore Your Promised Land Through Education

1. From this chapter, describe the differences between a foolish Christian and a successful Christian. *(page 39)*

2. How can you become a sharp or a sharper arrow in God's hands? How can you increase your credibility? *(page 40)*

3. Assess your training, education, and experiences in light of what you are discovering about your Promised Land.

   - Where do they mesh?

tion in the sight of God'" Luke 16:12, 15 NKJV.

"Before I formed you in the womb I knew you; Before you were born I sanctified you; I ordained you a prophet to the nations" Jeremiah 1:5 NKJV.

Use Your Gifts

"Every good gift and every perfect gift is from above, and cometh down from the Father of lights" James 1:17.

"Do not neglect the gift which is in you" 1 Timothy 4:14 AMP.

"Fan into flame the gift of God...Guard the good deposit that was entrusted to you " 2 Timothy 1:6-7, 14 NIV.

"Blessed be the Lord, who daily loadeth us with benefits, even the God of our salvation. Selah" Psalm 68:19.

"Delight yourself in the LORD and he will give you the desires of your heart" Psalm 37:4 NIV.

"'For I know the plans I have for you,' declares the LORD, 'plans to prosper you and not to harm you, plans to give you hope and a future'" Jeremiah 29:11 NIV.

"For unto every one that hath shall be given, and he shall have abundance: but from him that hath not shall be taken away even that which he hath. And cast ye the unprofitable servant into outer darkness: there shall be weeping and gnashing of teeth" Matthew 25:29-30.

"I beseech you therefore, brethren, by the mercies of God, that ye present your bodies a living sacrifice, holy, acceptable unto God, which is your reasonable service" Romans 12:1 NIV.

"He that is faithful in that which is least is faithful also in much: and he that is unjust in the least is unjust also in much" Luke 16:10.

Take Action

"And the things that thou hast heard of me among many witnesses, the same commit thou to faithful men, who shall be able to teach others also" 2 Timothy 2:2.

"Jesus gave them this answer: 'I tell you the truth, the Son can do nothing by himself; he can do only what he sees his Father doing, because whatever the Father does the Son also does'" John 5:19 NIV.

- Where do they intersect?

- Where do they oppose each other?

4. In your pursuit of the world's knowledge, prayerfully consider whether or not you have taken on the world's values and character. List changes you need to make. *(pages 43-44)*

5. List the kind of Kingdom values we must impose on the world.

D. Empty the Pews

If you have been warming a pew or involved only in housekeeping ministry, BREAK OUT!

Describe three things you can do immediately to shift to sphere-subduing.

1.

2.

3.

"By myself I can do nothing; I judge only as I hear, and my judgment is just, for I seek not to please myself but him who sent me" John 5:30 NIV.

"...I do nothing on my own but speak just what the Father has taught me. The one who sent me is with me; he has not left me alone, for I always do what pleases him" John 8:28-29 NIV.

"We do not want you to become lazy, but to imitate those who through faith and patience inherit what has been promised" Hebrews 6:12.

Pursue Education

"Blessed is the man who finds wisdom, the man who gains understanding" Proverbs 3:13 NIV.

"Every prudent man acts out of knowledge, but a fool exposes his folly" Proverbs 13:16 NIV.

"He made my mouth like a sharpened sword, in the shadow of his hand he hid me; he made me into a polished arrow and concealed me in his quiver" Isaiah 49:2 NIV.

"My people are destroyed from lack of knowledge" Hosea 4:6.

PART TWO

SHIFT STUDY:

Historical Perspective: George Washington Carver

The agricultural chemist George Washington Carver helped to rebuild the South after the American Civil War by developing crop rotation, which revolutionized agriculture and restored soil that had been depleted from decades of one-crop farming. He also developed hundreds of profitable uses for new crops including three hundred uses for peanuts.

Carver looked to meet needs. When textile dyes became scarce during World War I, he invented new dyes. He patented only three of the hundreds of products he developed. "God gave them to me," he said about his ideas. "How can I sell them?"

Born into slavery on the farm of Moses Carver, the young George was raised by Moses and his wife after abolition. No nearby schools would accept him, so at twelve years old Carver left home to pursue education, eventually graduating from what is now Iowa State University. He returned to the South at the invitation of Booker T. Washington to serve as the Director of Agriculture at Tuskegee Institute.

Foregoing the wealth that could have matched his fame, he derived his joy from serving society.[1]

Kingdom Values

"But the fruit of the Spirit is love, joy, peace, longsuffering, kindness, goodness, faithfulness, gentleness, self-control. Against such there is no law" Galatians 5:22-23 NKJV.

"Though I speak with the tongues of men and of angels, but have not love, I have become sounding brass or a clanging cymbal. And though I have the gift of prophecy, and understand all mysteries and all knowledge, and though I have all faith, so that I could remove mountains, but have not love, I am nothing. And though I bestow all my goods to feed the poor, and though I give my body to be burned, but have not love, it profits me nothing. Love suffers long and is kind; love does not envy; love does not parade itself, is not puffed up; does not behave rudely, does not seek its own, is not provoked, thinks no evil; does not rejoice in iniquity, but rejoices in the truth; bears all things, believes all things, hopes all things, endures all things. Love never fails. But whether there are prophecies, they will fail; whether there are tongues, they will cease; whether there is knowledge, it will vanish away. For we know in part and we prophesy in part. But when that which is perfect has come, then that which is in part will be done away. When I was

SHIFT PRAYER:

Father in heaven, I want to thank You that You are a God of purpose—nothing happens by accident according to You. Hence, I am not an accident, but You created me for a specific task on the earth. Now, Lord, lead me to my land of promise, I pray. Help me not to perish in the wilderness of confusion and personal gratification. Use me, Lord, to win back the earth for You, for the earth is Yours and the fullness thereof. Bless me, Lord, with the necessary grace to pay the price. In Jesus' name, Amen.

SHIFT MEDITATION:

"And I say to you, My friends, do not be afraid of those who kill the body, and after that have no more that they can do. But I will show you whom you should fear: Fear Him who, after He has killed, has power to cast into hell; yes, I say to you, fear Him! Are not five sparrows sold for two copper coins? And not one of them is forgotten before God. But the very hairs of your head are all numbered. Do not fear therefore; you are of more value than many sparrows.

Also I say to you, whoever confesses Me before men, him the Son of Man also will confess before the angels of God. But he who denies Me before men will be denied before the angels of God" Luke 12:4-9 NKJV.

REPEAT: My promised land is where my love and pain intersect, where they cross each other. My promised land is my personal cross where I represent the cross of Christ.

No individual has any right to come into the world and go out of it without leaving something behind.
~ George Washington Carver

[1] Adapted from materials at www.about.com and www.wikipedia.org

a child, I spoke as a child, I understood as a child, I thought as a child; but when I became a man, I put away childish things. For now we see in a mirror, dimly, but then face to face. Now I know in part, but then I shall know just as I also am known. And now abide faith, hope, love, these three; but the greatest of these is love" 1 Corinthians 13 NKJV.

SHIFT CHALLENGE 4

LEADER*SHIFT*

SHIFTING OUR MIND, *SHIFTING* THE CHURCH

What Is Ministry and Who Is the Minister?
John 4:33-39

Ministry is what Christians do as we bring our life and our sphere of influence under Kingdom rule and dominion. Ministry is not just preaching or teaching or working in the church. Ministry is not just singing or teaching Sunday School. Ministry is not just the apostle, prophet, evangelist, pastor, teacher. Ministry is not just religion.

In his letter to the Ephesians, Paul tells us that believers are to be trained to bring God to all areas of life (Ephesians 4:11-13). A street cleaner may bring more of God to people on the sidewalk and in their cars than other, more high-profile ministers. All who carry God are ministers. Every believer is a full-time minister. We can be busy outside the four walls of the church and shine for God wherever we are. Ministry is not necessarily what we do around the church but what we do *everywhere* to make our world and the earth come under the influence of the Kingdom (Revelation 11:15). Our work, job, or ministry are only the tools we use to advance the Kingdom, our platform from which we can better proclaim Kingdom values (Matthew 28:18-20). Ministry permeates our *lifestyle* (Matthew 28:18-20). Kingdom *lifestyle* is our goal.

The essence of the New Testament is that our very life is all about ministry (John 1:17-18; 2 Corinthians 3:1-3). Jesus demonstrated this lifestyle and teaching. People should be able to look at us and understand God, just as they did with Jesus. We are all disguised ministers. An engineer is a disguised pastor; a businessman is a disguised evangelist; a politician is a disguised apostle. All areas of life need ministry, and all Christians in all areas of life provide ministry.

SHIFT YOUR THINKING:

1. What does the term "Kingdom lifestyle" mean to you?

2. What areas are around you, outside of the church, that need ministry?

3. What do you think would happen to your community and country if every member views himself or herself as a minister?

STAINLESS
STEEL

Lesson Four

Embody the Nature of Our King

PART ONE

Read the book: Becoming Kingdom-Minded

Before you can rule in your promised land, you must be ruled by the Kingdom, transformed by the renewing of your mind, addicted to God. When you embody the characteristics and values of Christ the King and live by His teachings and principles, you actually bring the Kingdom of God to your world.

No longer a free moral agent, you are a reformer—created and called to permeate your spheres of influence to change culture, speak to society, cure social ills, and disciple with the whole truth. Reject the world's way and live by superior principles from a superior place. Your holiness and righteousness are your best testimony as a problem-chaser to show people that God is real. Embody the King's nature; be committed to the Kingdom.

A. Ruled by the Kingdom

1. Read aloud: *"I am the vine; you are the branches. If a man remains in me and I in him, he will bear much fruit; apart from me you can do nothing"* John 15:5.

***SHIFT* STUDY:**
You Will Learn

- When Christians make church the focal point of their lives and ministry, they burn each other like an oversalted dish and blind each other like a room full of spotlights.
- When a church loses focus, people get busy fighting among themselves. When our focus is not on finding our promised land and changing our society from right where we are, we start using kingdom resources to build our own kingdom.
- There is absolutely no use in having a big church without changing culture, speaking to society, and curing social ills.
- Egocentrism kills leadership because it shrinks their ambitions to the size of their own desires.
- The gospel of salvation, in isolation, will not change the earth. When you teach a halftruth, you destroy the truth.

- This world can only be properly managed by people who rule from a superior place and superior principles.

- We must work better and harder than anybody else. The Kingdom of God will work for us at the same level we are committed to the Kingdom.

- Only those who are increasingly filled with God's nature will become deliverers and saviors of their nation, community, and family. Love and help people before you ever try to influence them.

SHIFT SCRIPTURES:

Kingdom Mind-Set

"Now after John was put in prison, Jesus came to Galilee, preaching the gospel of the kingdom of God, and saying, 'The time is fulfilled, and the kingdom of God is at hand. Repent, and believe in the gospel'" Mark 1:14-15 NKJV.

"In this manner, therefore, pray: Our Father in heaven, Hallowed be Your name. Your kingdom come. Your will be done On earth as it is in heaven" Matthew 6:9-10 NKJV.

"Then the King will say to those on His right hand, 'Come, you blessed of My Father, inherit the kingdom

2. Do you personally tend to "remain in Christ" or do you mostly just hope He "remains in you"? *"You did not choose Me, but I chose you and appointed you that you should go and bear fruit, and that your fruit should remain, that whatever you ask the Father in My name He may give you"* John 15:16 NKJV.

3. If addiction to Christ were a disease, then based on your level of addiction to Christ today, what is your condition? Is your case terminal and permanent? Is it a mild case or a full-blown case?

B. The Church-Minded Church

1. Can a Christian make church too much of a focal point of life and ministry? *(page 51)*

   If so, how? What would be a solution?

2. Reread the pastors' joint statement of apology on pages 52-53.

   Describe the statement's impact on you.

Do you struggle with unforgiveness toward leaders of any kind who failed to release blessing and favor on you or who didn't acknowledge and support your call and dreams? Pray to release the past, and ask God to help you find new, encouraging relationships.

3. "Egocentrism kills leadership because it shrinks ambitions to the size of desires." *(page 58)*

   Meditate on or discuss this statement, then describe what you would see as a difference between these two leaders:

   Church-Minded

   Kingdom-Minded

   Which type of leader are you? Which do you aspire to be?

4. "A half-truth is a whole lie." How does this apply in your life? In your church? *(page 60)*

prepared for you from the foundation of the world" Matthew 25:34 NKJV.

"The earth is the LORD's, and all its fullness, The world and those who dwell therein" Psalm 24:1 NKJV.

Church Roles

"This is now the third time Jesus showed Himself to His disciples after He was raised from the dead. So when they had eaten breakfast, Jesus said to Simon Peter, 'Simon, son of Jonah, do you love Me more than these?' He said to Him, 'Yes, Lord; You know that I love You.' He said to him, 'Feed My lambs.' He said to him again a second time, 'Simon, son of Jonah, do you love Me?' He said to Him, 'Yes, Lord; You know that I love You.' He said to him, 'Tend My sheep.' He said to him the third time, 'Simon, son of Jonah, do you love Me?' Peter was grieved because He said to him the third time, 'Do you love Me?' And he said to Him, 'Lord, You know all things; You know that I love You.' Jesus said to him, 'Feed My sheep'" John 21:14-17 NKJV.

"So that you do not appear to men to be fasting, but to your Father who is in the secret place; and your Father who sees in secret will reward you openly" Matthew 16:18 NKJV.

Forgiveness

"This is how my heavenly Father will treat each of you unless you forgive your brother...from your heart" Matthew 18:35.

"[Now having received the Holy Spirit and being led and directed by Him] if you forgive the sins of anyone, they are forgiven; if you retain the sins of anyone, they are retained" John 20:23 AMP.

"When you forgive, release" John 20:22.

"Blessed is he whose transgressions are forgiven, whose sins are covered" Psalm 32:1 NIV.

"Not rendering evil for evil, or railing for railing: but contrariwise blessing; knowing that ye are thereunto called, that ye should inherit a blessing" 1 Peter 3:9.

"These things speak, and exhort, and rebuke with all authority. Let no man despise thee" Titus 2:15.

"The just man walketh in his integrity" Proverbs 20:7.

Chase Problems

"If any man will come after me, let him deny himself, and take up his cross, and follow me. For whosoever will save his life shall lose it: and whosoever will lose his life for my sake will find it" Matthew 16:24-25.

"But be ye doers of the word, and not hearers only, deceiving your own selves" James 1:22.

C. Rule from a Superior Place with Superior Principles

What principles make us kingdom minded? *(pages 61-64)*

1. Explain why holiness and righteousness can be the best testimony we have for showing people that God is real. *(page 63)*

2. Are you a "problem chaser"? Explain your answer. *(page 64)*

3. What role does "repentance" play in your life? *(pages 65-66)*

D. Learning to Love All Equally

1. How did this happen in Pastor Sunday's life? *(pages 66-67)*

2. Fill in: *(page 68)*

Love people! ______________ them no matter who they are or what they do. ______________ people regardless of their faults. __________________ them unconditionally. God's __________________ draws people, but our attitude often pushes them away. But if there is ____________, then that ______________ draws and keeps them. _________________ is the strongest bonding agent in the universe.

"Be thou an example of the believers, in word, in conversation (manner of life), in charity, in spirit, in faith, in purity" 1 Timothy 4:12.

"Neither as being lords over God's heritage, but being examples to the flock" 1 Peter 5:3.

Gain Wisdom

"Study to show thyself approved unto God, a workman that needeth not to be ashamed, rightly dividing the word of truth" 2 Timothy 2:15.

"If a man therefore purge himself from these, he shall be a vessel unto honour, sanctified, and meet for the master's use, and prepared unto every good work" 2 Timothy 2:21.

"Get wisdom, get understanding: forget it not; neither decline from the words of my mouth. Forsake her not, and she shall preserve thee: love her and she shall keep thee. Wisdom is the principal thing; therefore get wisdom: and with all thy getting get understanding" Proverbs 4:5-8.

"For Ezra had prepared his heart to seek the law of the Lord, and to do it, and to teach in Israel statutes and judgments" Ezra 7:10.

Reject Lies

"They exchanged the truth of God for a lie, and worshiped and served created things rather than the Creator – who is forever praised. Amen" Romans 1:25.

"They received not the love of the truth, that they might be saved" 2 Thessalonians 2:10.

"And judgment is turned away backward, and justice standeth afar off: for truth is fallen in the street, and equity cannot enter" Isaiah 59:14.

"Let us not love in word, neither in tongue, but in deed and in truth" 1 John 3:18.

"But you have received the Holy Spirit and he lives within you, in your hearts ... he teaches you all things, and he is the Truth" 1 John 2:27 TLB.

Love People!

"He that hath my commandments, and keepeth them, he it is that loveth me" John 14:21.

"If ye keep my commandments, ye shall abide in my love" John 15:10.

"Love is ... never haughty or selfish or rude. Love does not demand its own way" 1 Corinthians 13:4, 5.

"If you love someone you will always believe in him, always expect the best of him, and always stand your ground in defending him" 1 Corinthians 13:7 TLB.

______________________ preserves people in the kingdom of God. If they do something wrong, ______________________ them. Even if you do not like socializing with them, continue to ________________ them!

_________________ and help people before you ever try to influence them. _________________ them before they listen to you.

_____________________ them while delivering them from slavery. ________________ them while bringing them out of the world.

3. What is our "first commission"? *(page 68)*

4. "National transformation is today's assignment."

   How must you shift your thinking, your behavior, your goals, and your socialization in order to become deliverers and saviors of your family, community, and nation?

E. Applying *SHIFT* Words

1. Quietly, prayerfully compare these *SHIFT* words with your personality, behavior, and lifestyle.

Righteous	Reformer
Egocentric	Virtue
Smugness	Transparent

2. What two words would best describe the person you aspire to be?

_______________ _______________

3. If Jesus' followers embody the nature of their King, there will be no need to prove that we are Christians.

   If this shift were to happen in America tomorrow, how would your life change? Give examples from a variety of spheres (home, church, school, business, politics, etc.)

"May they be brought to complete unity to let the world know that you sent me and have loved them even as you have loved me" John 17:23.

"And walk in love, as Christ also hath loved us, and hath given himself for us an offering and a sacrifice to God for a sweetsmelling savour" Ephesians 5:2.

"Beloved, if God so loved us, we ought also to love one another ... If we love one another, God dwelleth in us, and his love is perfected in us" 1 John 4:11, 12.

"This is my commandment, That ye love one another, as I have loved you. Greater love hath no man than this, that a man lay down his life for his friends" John 15:12, 13.

PART TWO

SHIFT STUDY:

Historical Perspective: George Washington

U. S. President George Washington, the "father of the nation," came from a common Virginia upbringing with a defective education. He was educated into greatness by increasing responsibilities.

Washington had a fiery energy underneath a calm exterior, and a strategic mind that grasped how rumblings against taxation would certainly lead to war. A hero of the French and Indian War, Washington was unanimously selected as commander-in-chief of the American revolutionary forces. A role model for integrity, duty, honor, dignity, persistence, and patriotism, Washington was credited with preventing the Revolution from disintegrating, simply by virtue of his character.

Washington's influence made him the unanimous choice to preside over the Federal Convention that framed the American Constitution. When it came to vote for a president, the office had been cut to fit the measure of George Washington. He remains the only U. S. president to win 100% of the electoral vote.

Based on a belief that the value of religion was to benefit society, Washington's farewell address was one of the most influential statements of American political values and virtue. He said, "Reason and experience both forbid us to expect that national morality can prevail in exclusion of religious principle."[1]

SHIFT PRAYER:

Father, I come to You today with a repentant heart. I'm sorry that my focus has been wrong—about ministry and church instead of Your Kingdom. I, therefore, ask for Your forgiveness, Father. Change me today to become Kingdom focused. Let You and Your Kingdom become my motive, my vision, my aim, and my goal. Use me, Lord, daily as Your change agent, Your instrument of righteousness, peace, and joy. In Jesus' name, Amen.

SHIFT MEDITATION:

"You are the salt of the earth. But if the salt loses its saltiness, how can it be made salty again? It is no longer good for anything, except to be thrown out and trampled by men. You are the light of the world. A city on a hill cannot be hidden" Matthew 5:13-14.

Of all the dispositions and habits which lead to political prosperity, Religion and Morality are indispensable supports... Observe good faith and justice towards all Nations; cultivate peace and harmony with all. Religion and Morality enjoin this conduct.
~ George Washington

[1]Adapted from materials take in part from www.wikipedia.org and Encyclopedia Britannica, Eleventh Edition. New York: Encyclopedia Britannica Co.

SHIFT CHALLENGE 5

CHURCH*SHIFT*

SHIFTING THE CHURCH

The Ills of a Church-Minded Church
Matthew 6:33

When we are heavenly-focused, we are ruled by heavenly values. But when we are earthly-focused, we allow the earth to rule over us (Romans 6:14-16). Scripture admonishes us to focus on heavenly values (Colossians 3:1-5). God's plan is for those values to rule the earth because they are a superior value system.

The Church itself is to focus on the Kingdom, not on itself. The Kingdom was not founded to promote the Church, but the Church was founded to promote the Kingdom (Matthew 6:9-10). If the focus of the Church is itself, the Church is reduced to egocentrism and self-gratification, focusing just on the material and physical, rather than the spiritual and eternal (Matthew 6:25). An inwardly-focused Church suffers these evils:

1. Members focus on self-gratification rather than on taking responsibility for the earth (Galatians 4:1-4).
2. Tendencies of the flesh take over (1 Corinthians 1:10-17).
3. The church tends to function to meet the needs of the people instead of the people meeting the needs of God.
4. The salt loses its saltiness. Believers become ineffective in their society.
5. Light is hidden under a bushel. Light is concentrated in the church, not in the world.
6. Vision and direction are blurred because too much of the light intended for the world is in the church.
7. There is infighting in the church because members are not outwardly focused to win the world (1 Corinthians 3:1-7).
8. Division and church splits happen because people are not planted in their promised lands.
9. Leaders begin using the church to meet their own needs and use people to fulfill themselves.

10. Messages become ear-tickling, focusing on personal gain and fulfillment instead of on pursuing the Kingdom of God.
11. Members are motivated to satisfy self.
12. Resources are wasted because potential is conserved.
13. Religiosity and tradition hinder gospel power.
14. The society and nation are unredeemed.

As Christians, we are to focus on and be ruled by heavenly values. Contrary to the inwardly-focused church, the real purpose of the Church is to enforce the values of the Kingdom and Kingdom principles on earth.

SHIFT YOUR THINKING:

1. What values are exhibited by a church that is Kingdom-focused?

2. Read Matthew 6:9-10 and 25. In light of this study, do these verses take on fresh meaning for you?

3. Go through the 14 points on the list above and suggest the antidote. What would be the characteristics of a Kingdom-focused church? What kind of difference would that church make?

LESSON FIVE

GET TO WORK!

PART ONE

Read the book: Hard Work Leads to Success

Success in God's kingdom comes by putting kingdom principles into practice with great effort and diligence. The lack of plain hard work by righteous people has resulted in spheres of society suffering at the hands of the devil.

God expands the territory of hard-working people, but He won't automatically expand your borders. He gives you strength to conquer lands and exercise dominion over His creation through hard work.

God established work as a blessing for mankind and for His kingdom. Hard work is a key to

- subdue our Promised Lands
- develop the nature and character of Christ in ourselves
- successfully bring the principles of God into our spheres of influence and into the life of our nation.

SHIFT STUDY: You Will Learn

- Hard work is the wealth of a poor man.
- Hard work is one of the missing elements in many Christians' efforts.
- God has established work as a blessing for mankind and for His kingdom.
- Hard work is a key to subduing your own promised land.
- Jesus worked, and works still, because work was established by His Father as something good for humanity.
- By far the most important aspect of work is that it allows us to exercise dominion over all of God's creation.
- God is not obligated to bless people who don't work hard.

SHIFT SCRIPTURES:

God's Work

"But Jesus answered them, 'My Father has been working until now, and I have been working'" John 5:17 NKJV.

"And on the seventh day God ended His work which He had done, and He rested on the seventh day from all His work which He had done. Then God blessed the seventh day and sanctified it, because in it He rested from all His work which God had created and made." Genesis 2:2-3 NKJV.

"In all labor there is profit, But idle chatter leads only to poverty" Proverbs 14:23 NKJV.

"Jesus said to them, 'My food is to do the will of Him who sent Me, and to finish His work'" John 4:34 NKJV.

"Then He said to His disciples, 'The harvest truly is plentiful, but the laborers are few. Therefore pray the Lord of the harvest to send out laborers into His harvest'" Matthew 9:37-38 NKJV.

"Thus also faith by itself, if it does not have works, is dead...But do you want to know, O foolish man, that faith without works is dead?...For as the body without the spirit is dead, so faith without works is dead also" James 2:17, 20, 26 NKJV.

A. No Shortcut to Hard Work

1. Why is hard work one of the most neglected ingredients in many Christians' lives?

2. What are some consequences of this neglect?

B. The Blessing of Work

Fill in the blanks: *(page 76)*

1. Hard work and the ______________________________ rescued Sunday from a life of ________________.

2. Many believers incorrectly think hard work is a ______________, an ____________________________, a means of supporting themselves, or a means of ____________________________. *(page 76)*

3. Even worse, some see work as ___________________ ______________________ from their kingdom life. *(page 76)*

4. What is your opinion about working for God and advancing your own career? Are they mutually exclusive?

5. Name two things that God established work as a blessing for:

____

____

6. Explain this statement: "Anyone who does not work disgraces himself and steals from the wealth of those who do labor." *(pages 76-77)*

7. In the context of this chapter, describe "pitiful" people. *(page 77)*

"He who is slothful in his work Is a brother to him who is a great destroyer" Proverbs 18:9 NKJV.

"Then the LORD God took the man and put him in the garden of Eden to tend and keep it" Genesis 2:15 NKJV.

"Whatever your hand finds to do, do it with your might; for there is no work or device or knowledge or wisdom in the grave where you are going" Ecclesiastes 9:10 NKJV.

"Prepare thy work without and make it fit for thyself in the field; and afterwards build thine house" Proverbs 24:27.

Work is Profitable

"By much slothfulness the building decayeth; and through idleness of the hands the house droppeth through" Ecclesiastes 10:18.

"Wealth from gambling quickly disappears; wealth from hard work grows" Proverbs 13:11 TLB.

"This should be your ambition: to live a quiet life, minding your own business and doing your own work...As a result, people who are not Christians will trust and respect you, and you will not need to depend on others for enough money to pay your bills" 1 Thessalonians 4:11, 12 TLB.

"If any would not work, neither should he eat" 2 Thessalonians 3:10.

"Work brings profit; talk brings poverty!" Proverbs 14:23 TLB.

"What good is it...if a man claims to have faith but has no deeds?...For as the body without the spirit is dead, so faith without works is dead also" James 2:14-26.

"How long are ye slack to go to possess the land?" Joshua 18:3.

"Blessed is every one that feareth the Lord; that walketh in his own ways. For thou shalt eat the labour of thine hands: happy shalt thou be, and it shall be well with thee. Thy wife shall be as a fruitful vine by the sides of thine house: thy children like olive plants about thy table" Psalm 128:1-3.

Benefits of Work

"Wealth gained by dishonesty will be diminished, But he who gathers by labor will increase" Proverbs 13:11 NKJV.

"Do not love sleep, lest you come to poverty; Open your eyes, and you will be satisfied with bread" Proverbs 20:13 NKJV.

"He who tills his land will be satisfied with bread, But he who follows frivolity is devoid of understanding" Proverbs 12:11 NKJV.

C. Side Benefits of Hard Work

Name ten areas of life that are helped or improved by work: *(page 78)*

1.

2.

3.

4.

5.

6.

7.

8.

9.

10.

D. Aligning Your Mind-Set to Work

Name an action you can take to align your thinking and action with each of these statements.

- "As kings and priests of the earth, Christians are to do more work and be more diligent than anyone else." *(pages 78-79)*

- "God is not obliged to bless people who don't work hard." *(page 79)*

- "Hard work is absolutely critical to successfully bring the principles of God into our spheres of influence and into the life of a nation." *(page 79)*

"The soul of a lazy man desires, and has nothing; But the soul of the diligent shall be made rich" Proverbs 13:4 NKJV.

Work Mind-Set

"So then every one of us shall give account of himself to God" Romans 14:12.

"Thou madest him to have dominion over the works of thy hands; thou hast put all things under his feet" Psalm 8:6.

"Who then is the faithful and sensible slave whom his master put in charge of his household to give them their food at the proper time?" Matthew 24:45.

"His master said to him, 'Well done, good and faithful slave You were faithful with a few things, I will put you in charge of many things; enter into the joy of your master'" Matthew 25:21.

"And the Lord said, 'Who then is the faithful and sensible steward, whom his master will put in charge of his servants, to give them their rations at the proper time?'" Luke 12:42.

"Therefore if you have not been faithful in the use of unrighteous wealth, who will entrust the true riches to you? And if you have not been faithful in the use of that which is another's, who will give you that which is your own?" Luke 16:11-12.

"He that believeth on me, the works that I do shall he do also; and greater works than these shall he do; because I go unto my Father" John 14:12.

"I walked by the field of a lazy person, the vineyard of one with no common sense. I saw that it was overgrown with nettles. It was covered with weeds, and its walls were broken down. Then, as I looked and thought about it, I learned this lesson: A little extra sleep, a little more slumber, a little folding of the hands to rest—then poverty will pounce on you like a bandit; scarcity will attack you like an armed robber" Proverbs 24:30-34 NLT.

PART TWO

SHIFT STUDY:

Historical Perspective: John Calvin

John Calvin, the Church reformer from Geneva, Switzerland, was called "the father of America." American historian George Bancroft said, "He who will not honor the memory and respect the influence of Calvin knows but little of the origin of American liberty. The principles of Calvin...precisely his principles made this nation great."

Calvin and the Colonists' Biblically-based Christian worldview was based on the sovereignty of God and the final authority of Scripture. Calvin taught that Scripture is applicable to all of life, not just to matters of sin and salvation. His exposition of the Bible formed the political, economic, and religious life of America. Specifically, Calvin's theology formed the backbone of a representative system of government, is credited with the rise of the capitalistic economic system and gave birth to American education. Most of America's first colleges and universities—including Harvard, Yale, and Princeton—were founded by Calvinists.

Calvin's revolutionary principles, based on his belief in Jesus Christ as the sovereign Lord of all, stirred the blood, thrilled the heart, and gave birth to the freest nation in history.[1]

SHIFT PRAYER:

I thank You, Lord, that You are my example. Thank You for showing me the example and priority of work in life. Through work, Your purposes come to pass on the earth. I, therefore, pray that You'll take me wholly and use me to accomplish Your purposes on the earth. Father, take my will, take my strength, take my talent, and help me to maximize everything You've given me for Your plans and purposes on the earth. Thank you, Father, for hearing me. In Jesus' name, Amen.

SHIFT MEDITATION:

"Do you see a man who excels in his work? He will stand before kings; He will not stand before unknown men" Proverbs 22:29 NKJV.

"The hand of the diligent will rule, But the lazy man will be put to forced labor" Proverbs 12:24 NKJV.

"He who has a slack hand becomes poor, But the hand of the diligent makes rich" Proverbs 10:4 NKJV.

There is no work, however vile or sordid, that does not glisten before God.
~ John Calvin

[1]Adapted from Commentary from Dr. D. James Kennedy and *"The Man Who Founded America"* www.coralridge.org

SHIFT CHALLENGE 6

PEW*SHIFT*

SHIFTING THE PEWS, *SHIFTING* THE MEMBERS

The Kingdom-Driven Life
Matthew 6:25

People in the first century offered themselves to be killed by lions because of their willingness to defend their faith. While many Christians worldwide are still being martyred, today we also see many WIIFM Christians: *What's in it for me?* Often we see self-centeredness in what is supposed to be a Christ-centered life. When people are egocentric in their approach to God and the church, it fulfills Paul's prophecy about the last days (2 Timothy 3:1-5). The first sign of the end times is that people will love themselves more than God.

How can we allow ourselves to fall from being the most sacrificial religion in history to becoming the most comfortable and egocentric faith? At salvation, we are urged to deny self and make Christ our Lord, but often that is where our self-denial ends. Once saved, many focus on how to clean, sanctify, bless, heal, invest, prosper and, in general, take care of "self." Far from focusing on Christ, His Gospel and our glorious friendship with God, we shift our focus to me, me and more of me! Christ offers the opposite (Philippians 2:1-5).

Jesus taught us not to value anything in the world out of proportion, but always to make Kingdom passion our primary drive (Matthew 6:25, 33). He showed us that life is worth living only when it is lived for God. When ego, I, self, me, and mine are the motivating factors for our lives, not only do we get in trouble ourselves, but the whole church suffers. People begin to say, "If I am not going to be blessed or prayed for, why go to church?" Or, "I don't have a need this week, so I'm not going to the prayer meeting." These are sharp departures from the lessons taught by Paul and lived out by First Century Christians.

How can we become Kingdom-driven instead of self-driven or even church-driven?

Here are some ideas:

1. Remember each morning that the beauty of life is when you live for God and others (John 15:13). Let that be your motivating factor at the start of each day (John 3:16).
2. To be excited about living for the Kingdom, discover your promised land and your giftings that can make a real contribution each day. Focus on the area where God wants you to bless others.
3. Develop your gifts and character. To function effectively, we all need to carry the image of God, His character, and His values. Only then can people be drawn to us. Develop your gifts and multiply your talents.

SHIFT YOUR THINKING:

1. Study the three ideas listed. Do you wake up excited to have another opportunity to use your gifts for the world? What could help you remember to think about these each morning? What would keep you from doing them?

2. Do you run away from challenges or take them on?

3. If you lived in the first century, how far would you be willing to go for God? How far are you willing to go today?

Lesson Six

Promoted Through Persecution

PART ONE

Read the book: Thriving in Persecution

However unpleasant, persecution is never without purpose—kingdom purpose! God speaks to us in times of persecution. God trains and teaches us through persecution. We gain new skills and knowledge during persecution. Our character is revealed by persecution which then provides opportunity to grow the character of Christ within us.

Fear of persecution limits the Church and restricts the power of God to the four walls of our sanctuaries. Jesus asks us to go to the world and endure all it can throw at us—to do what He did.

Persecution is part of the Christian lifestyle. Expect it.

A. God Has Purposes for Persecution

1. How might Pastor Sunday's wariness of going to Russia have hindered God's purpose for his life?

SHIFT STUDY: You Will Learn

- A key to ruling your promised land is to enjoy the school of persecution.
- Some people want to be released from hardship before they have acquired the skills God wants them to have.
- Persecution reveals your character. It contrasts your selfish nature with the Kingdom nature God wants to work in you.
- Persecution gives us the perfect platform to overcome evil with good.
- Persecution is God's invitation to have a right response.
- Be faithful and let God judge your persecutor. It's OK to withdraw once you've been faithful.
- Fear of persecution has limited the church and hence the power of God to the four walls of our sanctuaries.

SHIFT SCRIPTURES:

Passing Tests

"He was in the beginning with God. All things were made through Him, and without Him nothing was made that was made. In Him was life, and the life was the light of men" John 1:2-4 NKJV.

"Now no chastening seems to be joyful for the present, but painful; nevertheless, afterward it yields the peaceable fruit of righteousness to those who have been trained by it" Hebrews 12:11 NKJV.

"But He knows the way that I take; When He has tested me, I shall come forth as gold" Job 23:10 NKJV.

"Before I was afflicted I went astray, But now I keep Your word" Psalm 119:67 NKJV.

"These things I have spoken to you, that in Me you may have peace. In the world you will have tribulation; but be of good cheer, I have overcome the world" John 16:33 NKJV.

What is wariness hindering you from doing?

2. Have you had a frustrating or disappointing situation(s) in your life that you complained about rather than prayed about? Explain what you could have done differently, or are doing differently today.

3. Read aloud:
"The Spirit of the Sovereign Lord is upon me, because the Lord has anointed me to preach good news to the poor. He has sent me to bind up the brokenhearted, to proclaim freedom for the captives and release from darkness for the prisoners" Isaiah 61:1 NIV.

   Pastor Sunday had never preached before and was only a young convert, six months in the Lord when he felt the Lord direct him to this passage. What does this passage mean to you personally? Explain your answer.

4. Have you been betrayed or negatively impacted for your Christian beliefs? How did you respond? How do you believe you should respond in the future?

B. Kingdom Nature Gets in You

1. How does persecution reveal one's character?

2. Fill in the blanks to complete these statements about the five reactions to persecution we are to have:

   - Our first reaction should always be __________ and ______________________________. *(page 87)*

   - Our second reaction is well shown in the Bible: But I say to you, ________________ your enemies, _______________ those who curse you, do ________________ to those who hate you, and pray for those who spitefully use and persecute you. *(page 88)*

   - Our third reaction is ______________________ for those who harm us. This connects us with God in the most powerful way possible. *(page 89)*

"There was a time when I wouldn't admit what a sinner I was. But my dishonesty made me miserable and filled my days with frustration ... until I finally admitted all my sins to you and stopped trying to hide them. I said to myself, 'I will confess them to the Lord.' And you forgave me! All my guilt is gone" Psalm 32:3-5 TLB.

"Blessed is the man who does not walk in the counsel of the wicked or stand in the way of sinners or sit in the seat of mockers. But his delight is in the law of the LORD, and on his law he meditates day and night. He is like a tree planted by streams of water, which yields its fruit in season and whose leaf does not wither. Whatever he does prospers" Psalm 1:1-3.

Build Character

"Ye have heard that it hath been said, Thou shalt love thy neighbour, and hate thine enemy. But I say unto you, Love your enemies, bless them that curse you, do good to them that hate you, and pray for them which despitefully use you, and persecute you; That ye may be the children of your Father which is in heaven: for he maketh his sun to rise on the evil and on the good, and sendeth rain on the just and on the unjust" Matthew 5:43-45.

"And unto him that smiteth thee on the one cheek offer also the other; and him that taketh away thy cloak forbid not to take thy coat also" Luke 6:27-29.

"Blessed are the peacemakers: for they shall be called the children of God. Blessed are they which are persecuted for righteousness' sake: for theirs is the kingdom of heaven. Blessed are ye, when men shall revile you, and persecute you, and shall say all manner of evil against you falsely, for my sake. Rejoice, and be exceeding glad: for great is your reward in heaven: for so persecuted they the prophets which were before you" Matthew 5:9-12.

"I discipline my body and make it my slave, so that, after I have preached to others, I myself will not be disqualified" 1 Corinthians 9:27 NAS.

"My son, despise thou not the chastening of the Lord, nor faint when thou art rebuked of him: For whom the Lord loveth he chasteneth, and scourgeth every son whom he receiveth" Hebrews 12:5-6.

"Who is he that condemneth? It is Christ that died, yea rather, that is risen again, who is even at the right hand of God, who also maketh intercession for us. Who shall separate us from the love of Christ? shall tribulation, or distress, or persecution, or famine, or nakedness,

- Our fourth reaction is freedom from __________. *(page 89)*

- Our fifth reaction: Finally, we need to be ____________________ and let God ________________ our persecutor. *(page 90)*

3. Why should we thank God for the tests?

4. Explain this statement: "Persecution gives us the perfect platform to overcome evil with good."

5. Describe the effects of fear...

on you personally:

on the church corporately:

C. School of Persecution

We are to expect persecution and rejoice in it as we grow into the stature of a mighty man or woman of God.

Think of situations and fears which hinder your ability to face, stand through, and rejoice in persecution.

1.

2.

3.

How can you practice the five reactions to persecution in each one?

This week, pray for God to promote you through the hardships you are enduring, giving you strength and confidence. Assess your growth as a mighty person of God. Write in a journal what changes you have made and what still requires attention.

or peril, or sword? As it is written, For thy sake we are killed all the day long; we are accounted as sheep for the slaughter" Romans 8:34-36.

"Therefore if thine enemy hunger, feed him; if he thirst, give him drink: for in so doing thou shalt heap coals of fire on his head. Be not overcome of evil, but overcome evil with good" Romans 12:20-21.

Use Persecution

"Strengthening the disciples and encouraging them to remain true to the faith. 'We must go through many hardships to enter the kingdom of God,' they said" Acts 14:22 NKJV.

"Am I now trying to win the approval of men, or of God? Or am I trying to please men? If I were still trying to please men, I would not be a servant of Christ" Galatians 1:10 NIV.

"You, my brothers, were called to be free. But do not use your freedom to indulge the sinful nature; rather, serve one another in love" Galatians 5:13 NIV.

"And be not conformed to this world: but be ye transformed by the renewing of your mind, that ye may prove what is that good, and acceptable, and perfect, will of God. For I say, through the grace given unto me, to every man that is among you, not to think of himself more highly than he ought to think; but to think soberly, according

as God hath dealt to every man the measure of faith" Romans 12:2-3.

"Nay, in all these things we are more than conquerors through him that loved us. For I am persuaded, that neither death, nor life, nor angels, nor principalities, nor powers, nor things present, nor things to come, Nor height, nor depth, nor any other creature, shall be able to separate us from the love of God, which is in Christ Jesus our Lord" Romans 8:37-39.

PART TWO

SHIFT STUDY:

Historical Perspective: Galileo Galilei

A Tuscan physicist, mathematician, astronomer, and philosopher, Galileo Galilei's quantitative experiments and systematic studies of motion paved the way for future scientists, including Isaac Newton. Albert Einstein called him "the father of modern science."

By improving on the telescope, Galileo discovered sunspots, a mountainous moonscape, and planetary evidence that caused him to support Copernicus' theory that the universe revolved around the sun, not the earth. Although he achieved worldwide fame and was a devout Catholic, the Church believed his views were damaging. Galileo argued that proper interpretation of Scripture would agree with observed fact, but the Inquisition disagreed and forced Galileo into house arrest.

Galileo persevered with writings that flew in the face of modern physics. He eventually contributed to the development of longitude, surveying tools later used by Lewis and Clark, a portable marine chronometer, the pendulum clock, the microscope, the understanding of sound frequency, and drew other ingenious sketches including a ballpoint pen.

Through his rigorous experiments and mathematical descriptions of the laws of nature, Galileo changed the world by putting forward the first law of motion and the Basic Theory of Relativity, later expanded by Newton and Einstein.[1]

SHIFT PRAYER:

Even though I might be hurting, I confess to You today that You are my strength, my hope, and my sustenance. I rely on You in my hour of weakness. Please give me the grace to pass through what I am now going through. Give me the persistence and tenacity to hold onto You, no matter the cost or price to be paid. Help me, Lord, never to quit or be tired of doing Your will and pursuing Your purpose for my life despite the trying circumstances. Help me, Lord, to learn all the necessary lessons I need to learn in this trying period of my life. Let Your name be glorified in my life Lord. In Jesus' name, Amen.

SHIFT MEDITATION:

"Blessed are you when they revile and persecute you, and say all kinds of evil against you falsely for My sake. Rejoice and be exceedingly glad, for great is your reward in heaven, for so they persecuted the prophets who were before you" Matthew 5:11-12 NKJV.

I do not feel obliged to believe that the same God who has endowed us with sense, reason, and intellect has intended us to forgo their use.
~ Galileo

[1]Adapted from materials at www.ChristianityToday.com and www.wikipedia.org

SHIFT CHALLENGE 7

CHURCHSHIFT

LET'S SHIFT THE CHURCH

The Kingdom Addiction
Matthew 6:9-10

God's Word tells us to be addicted to the ministry of the Kingdom (1 Cor 16:15). To be Kingdom-addicted means to be absolutely and totally consumed, dominated, and ruled by Kingdom purpose, values, and principles. To be Kingdom-addicted is to:

- surrender ourselves to the will of another—Christ—and to become led by the Spirit of God in our thoughts and actions.
- dedicate ourselves to promoting the values of the Kingdom whatever it may cost us, to work for its advancement.
- make the promotion and spread of the Kingdom our food, water, breath, treasure, and life (John 4:31-38).
- be overwhelmed by the personality and character of Christ Himself.
- demonstrate to the world and Satan that God's Kingdom is superior to the treasures of this world (James 4:4).
- live from a superior place in our thinking, mindset, and lifestyle (John 3:31).

Kingdom addicts strive daily to put on the nature and character of Christ who is the King of this Kingdom (Matthew 6:33). When we demonstrate Kingdom values by our daily lifestyle, the world is no longer able to mock us as fanatics. Instead, we impose the values of the Kingdom upon this perishing earth (Matthew 28:18-20). We prove by our lifestyle that God is superior to evil, love is superior to hatred, forgiveness is superior to vengeance (Romans 12:27), mercy is superior to judgment, honesty is superior to lying, trust is stronger than suspicion and doubt. These are the messages of the Cross.

The earth was created from a Kingdom prototype, so the earth has to function according to the values and principles of the Kingdom of God (Ephesians 4:17-18; Genesis 1:26-28; 1 Peter 2:1-2). Through our daily lifestyle as Kingdom addicts, we demonstrate that the values of the world cannot last, but that Kingdom values subdue the earth.

SHIFT YOUR THINKING:

1. Describe the symptoms of addiction, and relate that to the Kingdom addiction. Are you a Kingdom addict?

2. John 3:31- How do you understand living from the superior place as a Christian? Find the contrasts in earthly living vs. Kingdom living written above.

3. Can the earth and earth's systems withstand the power of the Kingdom and Kingdom principles? What could you do this week that would strengthen the earth's powers? What can you do this week that would strengthen the Kingdom's power over the earth?

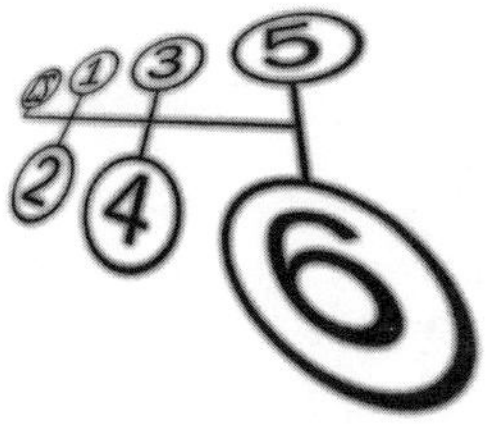

Lesson Seven

Find the Outcasts!

PART ONE

Read the book: Go to the Least of These

God usually starts at the bottom of society, serving the least, not the leaders. If you want to build the kingdom of God, serve the people around you who are considered the least important and the least valuable.

The destinies of many people depend on how you respond to God's direction for your life—to spread the good news! Ministry is really about touching people, not expecting people to go out of their way to come listen to you. Don't be part of the problem; make sure your understanding about church ministry is correct—become trustworthy with the down-and-outers, the outcasts, the unlovables, and the untouchables.

Love people with the love of the Lord, and you can change the world!

A. Give Up the Fight, and *SHIFT* Your Focus

1. Do you find it easy to obey God's change of direction or focus in your life? Or do you wrestle with God?

SHIFT STUDY: You Will Learn

- The destinies of many people depend on how you respond to God.
- God loves to serve those who are considered least in a society.
- Preaching and church ministries are just tools and instruments you can use but ministry is really about touching people.
- God won't entrust you with the greatest until He can trust you with the least.
- My breakthrough came when I left the pulpit and went to the streets to look for the outcasts.
- If you can love people with God's love, then you can change the world.
- To reach new heights in the Kingdom you must extend your hand to the depths and become a friend of the unwanted and unloved.

SHIFT SCRIPTURES:

Become a Servant

"Yet it shall not be so among you; but whoever desires to become great among you, let him be your servant. And whoever desires to be first among you, let him be your slave— just as the Son of Man did not come to be served, but to serve, and to give His life a ransom for many" Matthew 20:26-28 NKJV.

"But this I say: He who sows sparingly will also reap sparingly, and he who sows bountifully will also reap bountifully. So let each one give as he purposes in his heart, not grudgingly or of necessity; for God loves a cheerful giver. And God is able to make all grace abound toward you, that you, always having all sufficiency in all things, may have an abundance for every good work. As it is written: 'He has dispersed abroad, He has given to the poor; His righteousness endures forever.' Now may He who supplies seed to the sower, and bread for food, supply and multiply the seed you have sown and increase the fruits of your righteousness, while you are enriched in everything for all liberality, which causes thanksgiving through us to God. For the administration of this service not only supplies the needs of the saints, but also

2. Describe "reaper warriors." How can you become one? *(page 94)*

3. What was wrong with Pastor Sunday's vision to have a church full of rich and powerful people who would get saved and do great things for God? *(page 95)*

B. **Captivated by the Message of the Gospel**

"...And the common people heard him gladly" Mark 12:37 KJV.

1. Are you disillusioned over dejected derelicts in your life? *(page 95)*

   Has God pierced your heart for others?

2. Was Pastor Sunday's disappointment over Natasha normal? How did it turn around?

C. Outcasts Begin to Look Respectable

1. How do people living in the shadows of society become respectable? *(page 98)*

2. Fill in the blanks to illustrate how loving outcasts with the love of Christ changed Pastor Sunday's world in Kyiv. (pages 98-99)

   But when people came and felt the

   _________________________, they looked past

   their ___________________________, braved the

   _____________________ of their families, and

   made the ___________________________ their

   priority. In my first four years in Russia, I could

   not get any European saved, but now thousands

   were coming because our church was touching

   ___________________ people.

3. Serving "the least of these" is the primary concern of Pastor Sunday's church. It is their foundation. *(page 99)*

   When you think about your church, what is your primary concern?

is abounding through many thanksgivings to God" 2 Corinthians 9:6-12 NKJV.

"If there be therefore any consolation in Christ, if any comfort of love, if any fellowship of the Spirit, if any bowels and mercies, Fulfil ye my joy, that ye be likeminded, having the same love, being of one accord, of one mind. Let nothing be done through strife or vainglory; but in lowliness of mind let each esteem other better than themselves. Look not every man on his own things, but every man also on the things of others. Let this mind be in you, which was also in Christ Jesus: Who, being in the form of God, thought it not robbery to be equal with God: But made himself of no reputation, and took upon him the form of a servant, and was made in the likeness of men: And being found in fashion as a man, he humbled himself, and became obedient unto death, even the death of the cross. Wherefore God also hath highly exalted him, and given him a name which is above every name: That at the name of Jesus every knee should bow, of things in heaven, and things in earth, and things under the earth; And that every tongue should confess that Jesus Christ is Lord, to the glory of God the Father" Philippians 2:1-11.

Love Others

"He said to him, 'What is written in the law? What is your reading of it?' So he answered and said, 'You shall love the LORD your God with all your heart, with all your soul, with all your strength, and with all your mind,' and 'your neighbor as yourself.' And He said to him, 'You have answered rightly; do this and you will live.' But he, wanting to justify himself, said to Jesus, 'And who is my neighbor?' Then Jesus answered and said: 'A certain man went down from Jerusalem to Jericho, and fell among thieves, who stripped him of his clothing, wounded him, and departed, leaving him half dead. Now by chance a certain priest came down that road. And when he saw him, he passed by on the other side. Likewise a Levite, when he arrived at the place, came and looked, and passed by on the other side. But a certain Samaritan, as he journeyed, came where he was. And when he saw him, he had compassion. So he went to him and bandaged his wounds, pouring on oil and wine; and he set him on his own animal, brought him to an inn, and took care of him. On the next day, when he departed, he took out two denarii, gave them to the innkeeper, and said to him, "Take care of him; and whatever more you spend, when I come again, I will repay you." So which of

Is caring for people the foundation of your church or ministry?

Who are the "least of these" in your world?

D. Taking It to the Streets

Set aside quiet time to read and meditate on this passage:

"Then the King will say to those on his right, 'Come, you who are blessed by my Father; take your inheritance, the kingdom prepared for you since the creation of the world. For I was hungry and you gave me something to eat, I was thirsty and you gave me something to drink, I was a stranger and you invited me in, I needed clothes and you clothed me, I was sick and you looked after me, I was in prison and you came to visit me.' Then the righteous will answer him, 'Lord, when did we see you hungry and feed you, or thirsty and give you something to drink? When did we see you a stranger and invite you in, or needing clothes and clothe you? When did we see you sick or in prison and go to visit you?' The King will reply, 'I tell you the truth, whatever you did for one of the least of these brothers of mine, you did for me.'

"Then he will say to those on his left, 'Depart from me, you who are cursed, into the eternal fire prepared for the devil and his angels. For I was hungry and you gave me nothing to eat, I was thirsty and you gave me nothing to drink, I was a stranger and you did not invite me in, I needed clothes and you did not clothe me, I was sick and in prison and you did not look after me.' They also will answer, 'Lord, when did we see you hungry or thirsty or a stranger or needing clothes or sick or in prison, and did not help you?' He will reply, 'I tell you the truth, whatever you did not do for one of the least of these, you did not do for me.'

Then they will go away to eternal punishment, but the righteous to eternal life" Matthew 25:34-46 NIV.

Name some of the "least ones" you previously passed by. What do their faces look like? Have you passed by, not seen, ignored, been too busy for, been prejudiced against, been too fearful of, or just not wanted to be associated with them?

In prayer, ask God to transform your character so you can touch the down-and-outs of society so He can touch the greats of society through you.

these three do you think was neighbor to him who fell among the thieves?' And he said, 'He who showed mercy on him.' Then Jesus said to him, 'Go and do likewise'" Luke 10:26-37 NKJV.

"And Jacob was left alone; and there wrestled a man with him until the breaking of the day. And when he saw that he prevailed not against him, he touched the hollow of his thigh; and the hollow of Jacob's thigh was out of joint, as he wrestled with him. And he said, Let me go, for the day breaketh. And he said, I will not let thee go, except thou bless me" Genesis 32:24-26.

"Who can have compassion on the ignorant, and on them that are out of the way; for that he himself also is compassed with infirmity" Hebrews 5:2.

"For ye had compassion of me in my bonds, and took joyfully the spoiling of your goods, knowing in yourselves that ye have in heaven a better and an enduring substance" Hebrews 10:34.

"Finally, be ye all of one mind, having compassion one of another, love as brethren, be pitiful, be courteous" 1 Peter 3:8.

"But whoso hath this world's good, and seeth his brother have need, and shutteth up his bowels of compassion from him, how dwelleth the love of God in him?" 1 John 3:17.

God's Love

"But he, being full of compassion, forgave their iniquity, and destroyed them not: yea, many a time turned he his anger away, and did not stir up all his wrath" Psalm 78:38.

"But thou, O Lord, art a God full of compassion, and gracious, long suffering, and plenteous in mercy and truth" Psalm 86:15.

"The LORD is gracious and full of compassion" Psalm 111:4.

"Unto the upright there ariseth light in the darkness: he is gracious, and full of compassion, and righteous" Psalm 112:4.

"The LORD is gracious, and full of compassion; slow to anger, and of great mercy" Psalm 112:3-5.

"And when the Lord saw her, he had compassion on her, and said unto her, Weep not" Luke 7:13.

"And he arose, and came to his father. But when he was yet a great way off, his father saw him, and had compassion, and ran, and fell on his neck, and kissed him" Luke 15:20.

PART TWO

SHIFT STUDY:

Historical Perspective: Mother Teresa

A young Teresa enjoyed teaching at the Loreto convent school in eastern Calcutta but grew increasingly disturbed by the poverty surrounding her. In 1946 she felt a divine call to help. "I was to leave the convent and help the poor while living among them," she said. "It was an order. To fail would have been to break the faith."

In 1948 Mother Teresa ventured into the slums, initially starting an open-air school then tending to the needs of the destitute and starving. Her first year was fraught with difficulties which left her begging for food and supplies. Pressing on, she founded the Missionaries of Charity. Starting with just 13 members, they set out to care for those whom nobody was attending, including the sick and dying, the unwanted and unloved, the people who were a burden to society and shunned by others.

As her reputation grew in the world's eyes, Mother Teresa won the Nobel Peace Price, the Pope John XXIII Peace Prize, the Nehru Prize, the Balzan Prize and the Templeton and Magsaysay awards. Her work has blossomed into a worldwide network of branches of Sisters and Brothers who provide help to the poorest of the poor.[1]

SHIFT PRAYER:

Oh Lord, open my eyes to the least of Your children and creatures. I don't want to pass by the needy and suffering masses of my society anymore. I, therefore, ask Father for a compassionate heart. Please, Lord, give me the heart You gave the good Samaritan, so I would use Your resources for only those things You would like me to use them for, in Jesus' name, I pray. Thank You, Father, for granting me the grace. In Jesus' name, Amen.

SHIFT MEDITATION:

"The King will reply, 'I tell you the truth, whatever you did for one of the least of these brothers of mine, you did for me'" Matthew 25:40 NIV.

There is a terrible hunger for love. We all experience that in our lives - the pain, the loneliness. We must have the courage to recognize it. The poor you may have right in your own family.
Find them.
Love them.
~ Mother Teresa

[1]Adapted from www.wikipedia.org and www.nobelprize.org.

SHIFT CHALLENGE 8

PEW*SHIFT*

SHIFTING THE PEWS, *SHIFTING* THE MEMBERS

We Are Problem Chasers
Matthew 6:25

Christ's disciples sometimes complained about people. One day, they asked Jesus to send the people away because there was no food to feed them. Jesus responded by challenging the disciples to provide an answer themselves instead of sending away the people (John 6:40). The typical human response when people create a problem is not to get rid of the problem, but to get rid of the *people*!

Among the many lessons in the feeding of the multitude, Jesus gave a great lesson on how to live the Kingdom life by providing solutions for needy people. We are not to run from challenges or be intimidated into sending people away. *We* are *their* answer! As Kingdom people, we are uniquely equipped to provide answers. We hold Kingdom solutions to the challenges and troubles of our age (John 4:4). God is superior to all the challenges of life (1 John 5:4). We are people of God, people of faith. Our faith is a weapon that destroys all the evil of the world.

Jesus does not deny that challenges and sorrows abound in the world (John 16:33), but He *guarantees* we shall come out as victors, having already won the victory for us. We are not to shy away from challenges and problems, but to face them squarely and believe in faith for victory (Romans 1:17). We do not always like enduring temporary setbacks and occasional defeats, but the essence of our righteousness is the ability to live by faith, face challenges, and overcome them (2 Corinthians 4:18).

Troubles work miracles *in* us and give us the opportunity for miracles to come *through* us. Some Christians long for a time when they will be trouble-free. Never hope to see the end of challenges! We will never be free from them. The very existence of troubles encourages us to run to the Father. When the disciples could not cast out a demon one day, they came running back to Jesus (Matthew 17:14-18). Troubles help us know that God is more real and permanent than the troubles themselves. Evangelist Smith Wigglesworth once wrote, "If I didn't have problems, I looked for them."

You were uniquely and powerfully made as a new creation in Christ Jesus to produce answers and destroy problems. Whenever you provide one solution, immediately expect the next opportunity. Troubles are signs that we are alive and capable physically and spiritually to exert Kingdom influence. Instead of running *from* problems, we run *to* them. Kingdom principles supercede earthly strongholds. Darkness runs from light, and we are the light of the world. We need not run from the darkness, but simply turn on the light!

SHIFT YOUR THINKING:

1. List the advantages of troubles.

2. Have you ever wished that people with problems would go away? Who were they or what were their problems? Based on the reading above determine the solution to these problems to save (or help) the people.

3. "If I didn't have problems, I looked for them," is a challenging statement. What would the focus of your life have to be, in order to make this statement your own?

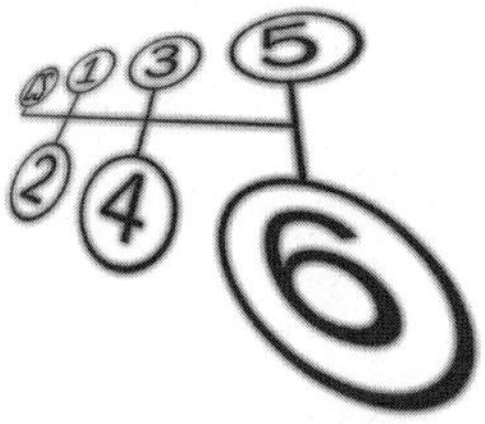

Lesson Eight

What to Do When Battles Come

PART ONE

Read the book: Learn to Fight!

Battle is the normal state of affairs for the believer. This is a contested planet. The devil won't just walk away from hard-earned territory.

God uses battle to train us. Psalm 105:19 NKJV says, *"Until the time that his word came to pass, the word of the LORD tested him."* Before the Word of God comes fully into your life, it will try you. It will test you. It will see what your reactions are to the battles. It will see if you are established in the Word and the revelation God has made available to you.

Every blessing, just like a coin, has two sides. Often we think that God's blessings protect us from tests. Just the opposite is true. With each blessing come temptations, tests, and opposition. As soon as God makes you stronger and multiplies your power and influence, you might as well brace yourself for the next wave of tests and battles.

We are attacked, not because God dislikes us, but because the devil doesn't like God blessing us. The time of battle, like the time of persecution, is the time to thank and praise God. It's time to get strengthened in faith and know that the blessings of God are stronger than the devil's attacks. "*...Greater is he that is in you, than he that is in the world*" 1 John 4:4.

SHIFT STUDY: You Will Learn

- Battle is normal as you move into your promised land. It means God is going to bless you if you persevere and stand your ground.
- There is no victory without battle. The devil won't just walk away from hard-earned territory.
- God uses battle to train us.
- With each blessing comes temptations, tests and opposition.
- It's important to remember that we are attacked not because God dislikes us but because the devil doesn't like God blessing us.
- God does not put us in battles without the proper weapons.
- God will sometimes allow problems and hardships in our lives in order to strengthen our spirits and teach us to put our trust in the Maker instead of putting it in our own strength.

SHIFT SCRIPTURES:

Battles Have Purpose

"Before I was afflicted I went astray, But now I keep Your word. The law of Your mouth is better to me Than thousands of coins of gold and silver" Psalm 119:67, 72 NKJV.

"For this is he who was spoken of by the prophet Isaiah, saying: 'The voice of one crying in the wilderness: "Prepare the way of the LORD; Make His paths straight."' Now John himself was clothed in camel's hair, with a leather belt around his waist; and his food was locusts and wild honey" Matthew 3:3-4 NKJV.

"Beloved, while I was very diligent to write to you concerning our common salvation, I found it necessary to write to you exhorting you to contend earnestly for the faith which was once for all delivered to the saints" Jude 3:1-3 NKJV.

It is the Lord's Battle

"Now thanks be unto God, which always causeth us to triumph in Christ, and maketh manifest the savour of his knowledge by us in every place" 2 Corinthians 2:14.

"Thine, O Lord, is the greatness, and the power, and the glory, and the victory, and the majesty..." 1 Chronicles 29:11.

A. Battles Are Normal

1. Pastor Sunday suffered lawsuits and death threats. Name some battles you have faced as a Christian, whether great or small.

2. Why do you think challenges are necessary to change our world?

3. How do battles of life make us into a better person?

4. How have you responded to battles?

5. Have you ever been in battle, yet able to sleep soundly and unworried? Why or why not?

6. How do you think you could respond to battles differently, now and in the future?

B. Passing the Test of Battle

1. Fill in: *(page 106)*

   Some Christians ______________the test of battle because they are ___________. They claim they are being ____________, but they are actually ______________ to fight battles because they are not dead to their own ___________.

2. How can each of the following result in losing a battle?

   - timidity

   - false humility

   - a desire for self-preservation

   - ego

   - not living totally for Christ

"O our God, wilt thou not judge them? for we have no might against this great company that cometh against us; neither know we what to do: but our eyes are upon thee" 2 Chronicles 20:12.

"...Be not afraid nor dismayed by reason of this great multitude; for the battle is not your's, but God's...Set yourselves, stand ye still, and see the salvation of the Lord with you...fear not, nor be dismayed...for the Lord will be with you" 2 Chronicles 20:15-17.

"For the LORD gives wisdom, and from his mouth come knowledge and understanding. He holds victory in store for the upright, he is a shield to those whose walk is blameless, for he guards the course of the just and protects the way of his faithful ones. Then you will understand what is right and just and fair—every good path" Proverbs 2:6-9.

"Wherefore take unto you the whole armour of God, that ye may be able to withstand in the evil day, and having done all, to stand. Stand therefore, having your loins girt about with truth, and having on the breastplate of righteousness; And your feet shod with the preparation of the gospel of peace; Above all, taking the shield of faith, wherewith ye shall be able to quench all the fiery darts of the wicked.

And take the helmet of salvation, and the sword of the Spirit, which is the word of God: Praying always with all prayer and supplication in the Spirit, and watching thereunto with all perseverance and supplication for all saints; And for me, that utterance may be given unto me, that I may open my mouth boldly, to make known the mystery of the gospel, For which I am an ambassador in bonds: that therein I may speak boldly, as I ought to speak" Ephesians 6:13-20.

Learn to Fight

"Blessed be the Lord my strength, which teacheth my hands to war, and my fingers to fight" Psalm 144:1.

"Wisdom strengtheneth the wise more than ten mighty men which are in the city" Ecclesiastes 7:19.

"Through thee will we push down our enemies: through thy name will we tread them under that rise up against us" Psalm 44:5.

"To this end I labor, struggling with all his energy, which so powerfully works in me" Colossians 1:29 NIV.

"No good thing will he withhold from them that walk uprightly" Psalm 84:11.

"Everyone who competes in the games goes into strict training. They do it to get a crown that will not last; but we do it to get a crown that will last forever.

3. "When the Israelite spies saw the people living in the Promised Land, they were fooled by their size. They were mortified and called them giants (Num. 13). In the same way, there are 'giants' on your way to ruling your promised land. There are problems, hardships, resistance, and persecution. Do not be afraid of them, because God Himself will fight for you." *(page 108)*

   List some of your "negatives"—both personal characteristics as well as circumstances around you—and list how they could be used for good by God:

   a.

   b.

   c.

4. Would God ever allow problems or hardships in your life on purpose?

   What purpose could they serve?

   What is required of you to win the battles of your life?

C. How Battles End

1. What is the "first result of battle"? *(page 110)*

How can this happen?

2. What is the next result of battle? *(page 110)*

Have you ever completely won a hard-fought victory? Explain.

3. What is the third result of battle? *(page 110)*

Name some instances in which you have seen positive come from what seemed only negative.

Therefore I do not run like a man running aimlessly; I do not fight like a man beating the air" 1 Corinthians 9:25-26 NIV.

"I have fought the good fight, I have finished the race, I have kept the faith" 2 Timothy 4:7 NIV.

"But thou, O man of God, flee these things; and follow after righteousness, godliness, faith, love, patience, meekness. Fight the good fight of faith, lay hold on eternal life, whereunto thou art also called, and hast professed a good profession before many witnesses" 1 Timothy 6:11-12.

Take Courage

"For God hath not given us the spirit of fear; but of power, and of love, and of a sound mind" 2 Timothy 1:7.

"The wicked flee when no man pursueth; but the righteous are bold as a lion" Proverbs 28:1.

"There is no fear in love; but perfect love casteth out fear: because fear has torment" 1 John 4:18.

"And David was the youngest: and the three eldest followed Saul...And David said to Saul, Let no man's heart fail because of him; thy servant will go and fight with this Philistine" 1 Samuel 17:14, 32.

Remember Battles Won

"I will speak of thy testimonies also before kings, and will not be ashamed" Psalm 119:46.

"And what shall I more say? for the time would fail me to tell of Gideon, and of Barak, and of Samson, and of Jephthae; of David also, and Samuel, and of the prophets: Who through faith subdued kingdoms, wrought righteousness, obtained promises, stopped the mouths of lions" Hebrews 11:32-33.

"Ye thought evil against me; but God meant it unto good, to bring to pass, as it is this day, to save much people alive" Genesis 50:17-20.

4. What is the fourth lesson of battle? *(page 111)*

5. When a battle comes, is it better to pray for God to shorten the battle or for Him to teach us to fight? Why?

D. God Will Give You Victory

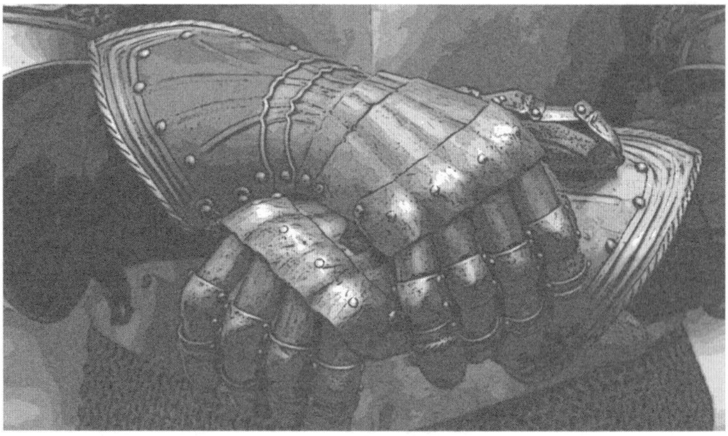

Pastor Sunday says, "To do nothing is to come to nothing."

1. What can you do this week to enhance your life and ministry calling?

2. Is it time to engage in a battle that you have avoided?

3. Name three ways you can prepare this week for coming battles as you SHIFT into your Promised Land.

   a.

   b.

   c.

PART TWO

SHIFT STUDY:

Historical Perspective: Abraham Lincoln

Abraham Lincoln warned the South in his first inaugural address, "You have no oath registered in Heaven to destroy the government, while I shall have the most solemn one to preserve, protect and defend it," thereby engaging the fight that became the American Civil War.

Born into ordinary circumstances, Lincoln struggled to eke out a living and an education. His constant reading, retentive memory, and belief in the Bible shaped his thinking and character. He persevered until he captured attention through his speeches while running for U. S. Senate. Losing the Senate, he won the presidency two years later.

With unparalleled leadership, Lincoln won many battles while winning the Civil War. He convinced the opposing party and the population to support the war. He united his own party's warring factions. He championed honesty and integrity, individual rights and human freedom. He issued the Emancipation Proclamation and promoted the Thirteenth Amendment to the Constitution to free America's slaves.

Lincoln even addressed factions within America's churches, promoting neither side but only God's will. Although never publicly stating his Christian beliefs, in his second inaugural address, he freely quoted Scripture and called on God, making him the most outspokenly "Christian" president in history.[1]

SHIFT PRAYER:

Heavenly Father, I pray You'll strengthen my hands for battle. Teach my hands to war as You taught King David. Grace me, Lord, to be able to glorify You both in good times and bad times. Deliver me, Lord, from soft-skinned Christianity. Help me to know that "greater is He that is in me than He that is in the world." I am thanking You ahead of victory, because Your Word says that You make us to triumph in all situations. I thank You that I'll surely come out of this stronger than I went into it. In Jesus' name, Amen.

SHIFT MEDITATION:

"Yes, and all who desire to live godly in Christ Jesus will suffer persecution" 2 Timothy 3:12 NKJV.

With malice toward none; with charity for all; with firmness in the right, as God gives us to see the right, let us strive on to finish the work we are in.
~ Abraham Lincoln

[1]Adapted from materials from www.whitehouse.gov; www.wikipedia.org and *A History of Christianity in the United States and Canada,* Mark Noll, (Eerdmans, 1992).

SHIFT CHALLENGE 9

LEADER*SHIFT*

LEADERS, LET'S *SHIFT*

Egocentric Leadership
John 21:14-15

Leaders are called to feed the flock and love the Lord. We do this in our homes, professions and communities. We love the Lord by serving Him and His Kingdom. We feed the flock by building the lives of the people entrusted to our leadership.

We are faithful to our local church, but not lovers of the Church. The Church is Christ's bride, and we are part of it. We love our "groom" Jesus, because we are part of His Church, but we don't love His bride. To love the Church more than Him or His Kingdom is a form of spiritual adultery. Pastors cannot be lovers of the churches they pastor.

We are lovers of God first, which is why we are willing to go even to another city or country if God says to serve in new harvest fields. The comfort we find in our home church does not hold us, because our love for our Lord is preeminent. Churches require lots of volunteers to be operational. We do not over-engage in church activities to the extent that we fail to feed our flocks at home. Jesus taught us to love Him and, out of that love, to love others and feed the flock (John 21:15-17).

True feeders cause the flock to run to expand the Kingdom. However, egocentric leaders kill a member's drive, passion and enthusiasm for the Kingdom by refusing to release that member to his or her Kingdom purpose and destiny. Egocentric leaders see their position as a means of survival or "making it big." They advance themselves instead of the Kingdom and are gratified when followers depend on them (John 10:11-18). Fearful that followers could become independent or self-sufficient, such leaders often accuse followers of division or rebellion (Galatians 2:20). They teach followers to finance their vision, but not to be financially independent and work in Kingdom enterprises outside the church (1 Corinthians 3:7-15). Egocentric leadership breeds egocentric membership. Members following such a leader's example will seek their own gain rather than exercising true leadership in service and stewardship. This breeds a "church ownership" mentality – as if tithing or serving means the church owes us something.

When we love the Lord and feed the flock, we focus on equipping others for service – our family members, home group members, employees and colleagues. We empower them to identify and act on their personal and individual vision, rather than binding them to work for or finance only our own vision. We help members occupy "housekeeping" duties in the Lord's house, but lead them also to find their promised land in their own sphere of influence in society. As we love the Lord and feed the flock, our followers run to find and fulfill their divine purpose.

SHIFT YOUR THINKING:

1. As a leader, what is your focus? To advance your ministry or create opportunities for those under you?

2. What are the two main goals of a leader? How does egocentric leadership fail to fulfill these goals? How does egocentric leadership produce egocentric followers?

3. Compare and contrast a government leader who is Kingdom-focused vs. egocentric. A teacher. A church music director. A businessman. A pastor. An athlete. A journalist.

Lesson Nine

Exert Your Power!

PART ONE

Read the book: You Are a Deliverer

To rule your Promised Land, you cannot rely on the goodwill of leaders. You must exert your power, become a godly leader, and actively take the land. We must all become Moseses.

To be a deliverer, you must identify with your nation. You need to believe that God cares for your nation as a whole. And you need to see yourself as an integral part of your nation.

Too many Christians see themselves as existing apart from their nation. They say they are citizens of heaven. That is true to a point, but it does not let us off the hook for completing our work here on Earth. It is impossible to be separate from your nation. God does not see you as an isolated individual with no connection to the society around you. You are part of your nation and are responsible for its sins or its righteousness. You are also part of your family and workplace and local body of believers. The way to be effective for the Kingdom is to identify with your nation, family, employer, and local community. Take responsibility for them and use your strength and all your skills to bring Kingdom principles.

SHIFT STUDY: You Will Learn

- It's not enough to have large numbers or justice on your side. God needs deliverers like Moses to lead people to victory using wisdom and power. To rule your promised land, you cannot rely on the goodwill of leaders.
- It's not enough to hide God's Word in your heart. You must speak for God in your place of influence.
- Sometimes speaking for God means confronting powerful rulers as Moses did. By confronting unrighteous leaders, you are doing them and your nation a favor.
- When people do God's will, the heart of the king belongs not only to God but also to the people of the country.
- We are actively to raise up God-fearing leaders from our own ranks to have their own impact on society.
- In today's world, ungodliness and evil point their dirty fingers at the Church of the living God, daring to challenge her.

- Every local Church can be a breeding ground for deliverers and Moseses. The Church is not for entertaining believers, but it is a place to raise up world changers and history makers.

SHIFT SCRIPTURES:

We Are Deliverers

"But we all, with unveiled face, beholding as in a mirror the glory of the Lord, are being transformed into the same image from glory to glory, just as by the Spirit of the Lord" 2 Corinthians 3:18 NKJV.

"By a prophet the LORD brought Israel out of Egypt, And by a prophet he was preserved" Hosea 12:13 NKJV.

"Then God said, 'Let Us make man in Our image, according to Our likeness; let them have dominion over the fish of the sea, over the birds of the air, and over the cattle, over all the earth and over every creeping thing that creeps on the earth'" Genesis 1:26 NKJV.

"He is the image of the invisible God, the firstborn over all creation" Colossians 1:15 NKJV.

A. Actively Taking the Land

1. If you chose not to take part in the first march of Pastor Sunday's church, when there were only 3,000 people and an uncertain outcome, would you have changed your mind for the second march with 20,000?

2. What would have made the difference for you?

3. What point is Pastor Sunday making when he states that we cannot rely on the "goodwill of leaders"? *(page 117)*

   Do you agree? Explain why.

B. Moses did five things to free his nation.
Name them: *(pages 117-126)*

a.

b.

c.

d.

e.

1. Read Jeremiah 29:7 in your favorite Bible version.

   The New King James Version quotes: *"And seek the peace of the city where I have caused you to be carried away captive, and pray to the Lord for it; for in its peace you will have peace."*

   After completing more than half of this study, what does this passage of Scripture now mean to you?

2. Fill in the blanks: *(page 118)*

   In other words, don't try to ______________

   yourself from working for the good of your nation,

   because God has ____________________

   your ______________ with its ______________.

Divine Power

'The kingdom of God does not come with observation; nor will they say, "See here!" or "See there!" For indeed, the kingdom of God is within you'" Luke 17:20-21 NKJV.

"As His divine power has given to us all things that pertain to life and godliness, through the knowledge of Him who called us by glory and virtue, by which have been given to us exceedingly great and precious promises, that through these you may be partakers of the divine nature, having escaped the corruption that is in the world through lust" 2 Peter 1:3-4 NKJV.

"Love has been perfected among us in this: that we may have boldness in the day of judgment; because as He is, so are we in this world" 1 John 4:17 NKJV.

"Who shall not fear You, O Lord, and glorify Your name? For You alone are holy. For all nations shall come and worship before You, For Your judgments have been manifested" Revelations 15:4 NKJV.

Insult of Sin

"But let your 'Yes' be 'Yes,' and your 'No,' 'No.' For whatever is more than these is from the evil one" Matthew 5:37 NKJV.

"And I fell down before the LORD, as at the first, forty days and forty nights; I neither ate bread nor

drank water, because of all your sin which you committed in doing wickedly in the sight of the LORD, to provoke Him to anger" Deuteronomy 9:18 NKJV.

"Then Moses returned to the LORD and said, "Oh, these people have committed a great sin, and have made for themselves a god of gold!" Exodus 32:31 NKJV.

"So he was there with the LORD forty days and forty nights; he neither ate bread nor drank water. And He wrote on the tablets the words of the covenant, the Ten Commandments" Exodus 34:28 NKJV.

"Afterward Moses and Aaron went in and told Pharaoh, 'Thus says the LORD God of Israel: "Let My people go, that they may hold a feast to Me in the wilderness"'" Exodus 5:1 NKJV.

Be Bold

"Then they will heed your voice; and you shall come, you and the elders of Israel, to the king of Egypt; and you shall say to him, 'The LORD God of the Hebrews has met with us; and now, please, let us go three days' journey into the wilderness, that we may sacrifice to the LORD our God'" Exodus 3:18 NKJV.

"O thou that hearest prayer, unto thee shall all flesh come" Psalm 65:2.

There are no exceptions for believers who are trying to follow God over in their own little corner. No, it's your ______________________ to make sure ______________ and ______________ ______________ come.

3. Pastor Sunday names the economy, political problems, ungodliness in entertainment, sports, and business. What other areas of your society need to be "fixed"?

   a.

   b.

   c.

   d.

4. In what ways can you speak for God? *(page 120)*

5. Name some decisions you can make that will: *(page 121)*

   Deliver People:

   Enslave People:

6. Pharoah is a symbol of anyone who keeps people from serving God. Name some "Pharoahs" or "Pharoah" positions that people take in your community or nation. *(page 121)*

7. We are "agents of change." Who are some leaders that God has raised up around you? *(page 123)*

8. How could you become one such leader?

9. Name six ways that Kingdom leadership is different from worldly leadership: *(page 124-126)*

   a.

   b.

   c.

   d.

   e.

   f.

"The king's heart is in the hand of the LORD, as the rivers of water: he turneth it whithersoever he will" Proverbs 21:1.

Build Character

"The good influence of godly citizens causes a city to prosper, but the moral decay of the wicked drives it downhill" Proverbs 11:11 TLB.

"Without wise leadership, a nation is in trouble" Proverbs 11:14 TLB.

"Beware of false prophets, which come to you in sheep's clothing, but inwardly they are ravening wolves. Ye shall know them by their fruits. Matthew 7:15-16.

"When there is moral rot within a nation, its government topples easily; but with honest, sensible leaders there is stability" Proverbs 28:2 TLB.

"With good men in authority, the people rejoice; but with the wicked in power, they groan" Proverbs 29:2 TLB.

"Moreover it is required in stewards, that a man be found faithful" 1 Corinthians 4:2.

Serve Others

"Now I want you to be leaders also in the spirit of cheerful giving...his is one way to prove your love is real, that it goes beyond mere words" 2 Corinthians 8:7, 8 TLB.

"Then said he to the multitude that came forth to be baptized of him, O generation of vipers...Bring forth therefore fruits worthy of repentance... the axe is laid unto the root of the trees: every tree therefore which bringeth not forth good fruit is hewn down, and cast into the fire. And the people asked...What shall we do then? He answereth...He that hath two coats, let him impart to him that hath none; and he that hath meat, let him do likewise...Exact no more than that which is appointed you...Do violence to no man, neither accuse any falsely; and be content with your wages" Luke 3:7-14.

God's Word

"The words that I speak...they are spirit, and they are life" John 6:63

"All scripture is given by inspiration of God... That the man of God may be perfect... furnished unto all good works" 2 Timothy 3:16, 17.

C. Read Isaiah 59:14-16 in your favorite version.

1. Does God use angels to do a man's work? *(page 128)*

2. Who does God use? *(page 128)*

3. Whom does God call "a man"? *(page 129)*

4. In your own words, define what it means to be "a man" or "a woman" in God's eyes. *(page 129)*

5. In what ways have you fulfilled God's purpose for creating "a man" or "a woman"? In what ways have you not fulfilled it?

D. Call to Action

1. What forms of ungodliness are hard for you to accept?

2. What forms of ungodliness are easy for you to ignore?

3. To become more sensitive to ungodliness, name three things you will do this week:

4. Name three things you will stop doing this week:

5. In what sphere are you to be a Moses?

6. How can your pastor help you become a Moses?

God's Spirit

"But the Helper, the Holy Spirit, whom the Father will send in My name, He will teach you all things, and bring to your remembrance all things that I said to you... However, when He, the Spirit of truth, has come, He will guide you into all truth; for He will not speak on His own authority, but whatever He hears He will speak; and He will tell you things to come" John 14:26; 16:13 NKJV.

"If ye then, being evil, know how to give good gifts unto your children: how much more shall your heavenly Father give the Holy Spirit to them that ask him?" Luke 11:13.

"But the anointing which you have received from Him abides in you, and you do not need that anyone teach you; but as the same anointing teaches you concerning all things, and is true, and is not a lie, and just as it has taught you, you will abide in Him" 1 John 2:27 NKJV.

Through His wisdom

"If any of you lack wisdom, let him ask of God" James 1:5.

"But of Him you are in Christ Jesus, who became for us wisdom from God—and righteousness and sanctification and redemption" 1 Corinthians 1:30.

PART TWO

SHIFT STUDY:

Historical Perspective: Harriet Tubman

Reverently called "Moses," Harriet Tubman was the most famous leader of the Underground Railroad, an elaborate series of houses, tunnels, and roads that aided slaves escaping to freedom before abolition. Tubman was born into abusive slavery before she escaped through the Underground Railroad.

After Congress made it illegal to help a runaway slave, Tubman realized she had the ability to help others. On her first Underground Railroad expedition, she threaded her way through backwoods and returned with her sister and her sister's children. Before the Civil War, Tubman traveled to the South 18 times, bringing close to 300 slaves to freedom, including her own parents.

Thomas Wentworth Higginson wrote in a letter from 1859, "a more ordinary specimen of humanity could hardly be found among the most unfortunate-looking farm hands of the South. Yet in point of courage, shrewdness, and disinterested exertions to rescue her fellow-man, she was without equal."

As her reputation grew, Southerners offered huge rewards for her capture. Tubman was never caught and never lost a slave to the Southern militia. Her courage to pursue her dream of freedom made Harriet Tubman a national hero.[1]

SHIFT PRAYER:

According to Your Word, oh Lord, You are always looking for someone who can take responsibility for himself or herself and demonstrate this type of selfless abandonment by taking responsibility for our world. Father, this grace I covet and desire. Make it mine, Lord. In Jesus' name, Amen.

SHIFT MEDITATION:

"By a prophet the LORD brought Israel out of Egypt, And by a prophet he was preserved" Hosea 12:13 NKJV.

"Like Moses, no one is sent to this earth without a mission. We are all called to be a Moses to a particular area of life, bringing deliverance to our generation."
~ Sunday Adelaja

Every great dream begins with a dreamer. Always remember, you have within you the strength, the patience, and the passion to reach for the stars to change the world.
~ Harriet Tubman

[1]Adapted from materials take in part from www.wikipedia.org and www.civilwarhome.com

SHIFT CHALLENGE 10

PEW*SHIFT*

SHIFT YOURSELF BEFORE YOU CAN *SHIFT* YOUR WORLD

You Must Be Ruled by the Kingdom Before You Can Rule in the Kingdom
Matthew 6:33

The Kingdom of God must first triumph *in* us before it can triumph *through* us. Our most important ministry is making sure our character conforms to the image of Christ (Romans 12:1, 2). Character is more important than the gift. The fruit of the Spirit is more important than the anointing of the Spirit.

Many earnest, well-meaning people who want to carry and manifest the Kingdom of God fail for a single reason: They don't understand that they must first be ruled *by* the Kingdom of God before they can rule *in* the Kingdom of God. In order to impact, we must first be impacted. To change, we must first be changed.

The Kingdom is the King's domain. Without Him there is no domain. The King's personality and nature must become ours before we can be ambassadors of the influence of His Kingdom (Matthew 6:33). Our top priority is to reflect the image of God (Ephesians 5:1-2). We must put on the King's image before we can rule for Him in His domain (Genesis 1:27).

We are to mold our lives after God's personality. We need to allow God to change us into His nature before we can be effective for Him (John 15:5). We need prayers and solitude in the Word just like trees need soil or fish need water to survive. The source sustains the product. Our source is God. We need Him in order to work for Him (Galatians 5:21-22).

God is looking for a physical expression through whom He can communicate Himself to the physical world of flesh and blood (Hebrews 10:5-7; Romans 12:1-2). The Word of God did not communicate as much to the physical world until it took on physical flesh. Jesus was able to reveal God because He had God's righteousness and He hated sin. He was anointed above others (Hebrews 1:9; Colossians 1:15).

We are called to make God become flesh again through our lifestyle. We take God from the invisible to the visible and manifest Him in our mortal flesh as Christ did (John 1:14). We carry Christ with us wherever we go. People need the God we carry. Our job is to spend time with Him so we manifest His Kingdom, then step out confidently, doing our best to make an impact for Christ. The world is waiting for you to begin to rule in the Kingdom.

SHIFT YOUR THINKING:

1. What is meant by the statement: "Character is more important than the gift. The fruit of the Spirit is more important than the anointing of the Spirit." In what ways can you improve your character? In what ways can you exhibit more of the fruits of the Spirit?

2. Who is the actual ruler of the Kingdom of God? What role do the servants of the King have in the Kingdom? Why is it important for them to reflect the image of the King?

3. How can you be ruled *by* the Kingdom of God? How will prayer and the Word change you into God's image? How will this cause you to reflect Christ in your daily life?

Lesson Ten

Let's Get Practical!

PART ONE

Read the book: Imposing the Kingdom on the Culture

In twelve years, two million people have come to Christ at the altar of our church. We thank God that we are being used to win the lost, but the truly amazing thing is that this has not taken place through evangelism, crusades, or traditional methods of sharing the gospel. Rather, people have come to the church and come to Christ because of the example of many thousands of Christians putting Kingdom principles to work outside of the church.

The heart of our discovery is that you don't need to promote religion or church for people to want to come to Christ. Rather, Kingdom principles will draw people. You don't even have to mention anything spiritual or religious—in fact, it's sometimes better not to. When you take God's principles into society, they simply work. They draw attention and people begin to inspect who you are, what motivates you, and what is the philosophy behind your work. Then they discover the kingdom within you, and they become convinced of its truth because they've seen it in action.

SHIFT STUDY: You Will Learn

- Principles unite, but religiosity divides. It is far better to emphasize the integrity of God's Kingdom principles and patterns rather than the spirituality of your particular Christian experience.
- You can bring Kingdom principles to the public sphere in a secular package and receive a far wider hearing.
- Eventually, Kingdom principles will dethrone the kingdom of darkness, like the mustard plant that crowds out other plants.
- By creating models for solving social problems, you inspire others to do the same. Instead of bemoaning the state of our nation, we take responsibility, create programs, register organizations, and start a movement.
- When believers occupy every sphere of life, the government can't do much. By promoting Kingdom principles, we also keep our foot in the door of power, lest the door close.

- God is organized and He pays attention to small things. Without structure, management, and organization, no miracle will bear lasting fruit. The programs that have been most effective in the world have been led by organized people.

- The Kingdom comes to others through your passion and gifting.

SHIFT SCRIPTURES:

Know Kingdom Principles

"He said to him, 'What is written in the law? What is your reading of it?' So he answered and said, 'You shall love the LORD your God with all your heart, with all your soul, with all your strength, and with all your mind,' and 'your neighbor as yourself.' And He said to him, 'You have answered rightly; do this and you will live'" Luke 10:26-28 NKJV.

"But the fruit of the Spirit is love, joy, peace, longsuffering, kindness, goodness, faithfulness, gentleness, self-control. Against such there is no law" Galatians 5:22-23 NKJV.

"For the kingdom of God is not eating and drinking, but righteousness and peace and joy in the Holy Spirit" Romans 14:17 NKJV.

A. Kingdom Principles

1. What are some Kingdom principles that you know?

2. Where could you begin to teach these Kingdom principles?

3. Explain in your own words, "Principles unite, religiosity divides." *(page 135)*

4. What is the best way to teach Kingdom principles, by preaching or by personal example? Explain.

B. Creating strategies

1. What purpose is served by forming an "NGO" or "non-government organization"? *(page 136)*

2. Name 3 powerful NGOs that you know about:

   a.

   b.

   c.

3. Do you know how each one started? What was its purpose in forming?

4. Pastor Sunday listed the following needs that his congregation discovered they could meet. Read these and add five more needs in your own community: *(page 138)*

   Smoking
   Teenage Pregnancy
   Alcohol
   Legal Aid
   Feeding Centers for Hungry
   Medical Help
   Street Children
   High Schools: Purpose and Responsible Living Classes
   Drugs
   Homeless
   Corruption
   Violence
   Pornography
   Lobbying Government

   a.

   b.

   c.

   d.

   e.

5. Fill In: *(page 137)*

   As you begin to think of what you might do to change society, remember that ________________ is the solution, but it's OK to present the solution in the way you are allowed, which means emphasizing principles, not ______________. You are __________________ representative. Just by being in a _________________, God is there.

"Then the mother of Zebedee's sons came to Him with her sons, kneeling down and asking something from Him. And He said to her, 'What do you wish?' She said to Him, 'Grant that these two sons of mine may sit, one on Your right hand and the other on the left, in Your kingdom.' But Jesus answered and said, 'You do not know what you ask. Are you able to drink the cup that I am about to drink, and be baptized with the baptism that I am baptized with?' They said to Him, 'We are able.' So He said to them, 'You will indeed drink My cup, and be baptized with the baptism that I am baptized with; but to sit on My right hand and on My left is not Mine to give, but it is for those for whom it is prepared by My Father.' And when the ten heard it, they were greatly displeased with the two brothers. But Jesus called them to Himself and said, 'You know that the rulers of the Gentiles lord it over them, and those who are great exercise authority over them. Yet it shall not be so among you; but whoever desires to become great among you, let him be your servant. And whoever desires to be first among you, let him be your slave—just as the Son of Man did not come to be served, but to serve, and to give His life a ransom for many'" Matthew 20:20-28 NKJV.

Impose the Kingdom

"Thy kingdom come, Thy will be done, as in heaven, so in earth" Luke 11:2.

"And saying, Repent (think differently; change your mind, regretting your sins and changing your conduct), for the kingdom of heaven is at hand" Matthew 3:2 AMP.

"I will worship toward Your holy temple, And praise Your name For Your lovingkindness and Your truth; For You have magnified Your word above all Your name" Psalm 138:2 NKJV.

"The Lord is good, a strong hold in the day of trouble; and he knoweth them that trust in him" Nahum 1:7.

"When we were children, we were in slavery under the basic principles of the world. But when the time had fully come, God sent his Son, born of a woman, born under law, to redeem those under law, that we might receive the full rights of sons. Because you are sons, God sent the Spirit of his Son into our hearts, the Spirit who calls out, 'Abba, Father.' So you are no longer a slave, but a son; and since you are a son, God has made you also an heir. Formerly, when you did not know God, you were slaves to those who by nature are not gods. But now that you know God—or rather are known by God—how

You have the anointing and the Kingdom ________________. Bring it to people in a way you are allowed to. Don't deny them ________________ answers just because you can't speak the ________________ ____________. Eventually, Kingdom principles will ________________ the kingdom of darkness, like the mustard plant that crowds out other plants. But every big goal starts out ________________. You start by doing what you ________________. Give it time to spread simply and naturally through you.

6. What will happen to others around you when they see you create a solution to a social problem? *(page 138)*

7. When believers start occupying every sphere of society, what happens to the Church? *(pages 138-139)*

8. What do Christians have that talk show hosts do not have? *(page 139)*

9. "We need to see every position of influence in society as a Christian assignment." *(page 140)*

   Explain your thoughts about this statement.

C. Getting Organized

1. In the story of Jesus feeding the multitude, what is Pastor Sunday's perspective on gathering the leftover food? *(page 141)*

2. Have you ever seen a good idea doomed by poor management? Or an organization that failed due to poor management?

3. Pastor Sunday said he was ignorant when he first became a pastor. Name two things he thought he needed to know or have: *(page 142)*

   a.

   b.

   Name one thing he now calls one-half of his success: *(page 142)*

is it that you are turning back to those weak and miserable principles? Do you wish to be enslaved by them all over again?" Galatians 4:3-9 NIV.

"Beware lest any man spoil you through philosophy and vain deceit, after the tradition of men, after the rudiments of the world, and not after Christ" Colossians 2:8.

"Except the Lord build the house, they labour in vain that build it" Psalm 127:1.

Provide Answers

"For we are his workmanship, created in Christ Jesus unto good works, which God hath before ordained that we should walk in them" Ephesians 2:10.

"But thanks be to God, who always leads us in triumphal procession in Christ and through us spreads everywhere the fragrance of the knowledge of him. For we are to God the aroma of Christ among those who are being saved and those who are perishing. To the one we are the smell of death; to the other, the fragrance of life. And who is equal to such a task? Unlike so many, we do not peddle the word of God for profit. On the contrary, in Christ we speak before God with sincerity, like men sent from God" 2 Corinthians 2:14-17 NIV.

"In everything I did, I showed you that by this kind of hard work we must

help the weak, remembering the words the Lord Jesus himself said: 'It is more blessed to give than to receive'" Acts 20:35 NIV.

"Make it your ambition to lead a quiet life, to mind your own business and to work with your hands, just as we told you, so that your daily life may win the respect of outsiders and so that you will not be dependent on anybody" 1 Thessalonians 4:9-12 NIV.

"...As God's chosen people, holy and dearly loved, clothe yourselves with compassion, kindness, humility, gentleness and patience. Bear with each other...Forgive as the Lord forgave you...put on love, which binds them all together in perfect unity. Let the peace of Christ rule in your hearts, since as members of one body you were called to peace. And be thankful. Let the word of Christ dwell in you richly as you teach and admonish one another with all wisdom... with gratitude in your hearts to God. And whatever you do, whether in word or deed, do it all in the name of the Lord Jesus, giving thanks to God the Father through him" Colossians 3:12-17 NIV.

4. Name the "Seven Spheres of Influence" Pastor Sunday identified: *(pages 143-144)*

   a.

   b.

   c.

   d.

   e.

   f.

   g.

D. Bring It Home!

1. Which one of the Seven Spheres of Influence excites you the most?

   What are you going to do about it?

2. Which are the next two you find most interesting?

   Why?

3. How can your passion and giftings be used in the sphere of society that most intrigues you to maximize the Kingdom of God?

4. Is it too late for you to start using your passion and giftings? What can you begin to do? *(page 144)*

5. What model would best suit your work in the sphere that interests you?

6. Has anyone ever done it before in history? Who? What made them succeed?

7. What can you learn from them?

"Let no corrupt word proceed out of your mouth, but what is good for necessary edification, that it may impart grace to the hearers. And do not grieve the Holy Spirit of God, by whom you were sealed for the day of redemption... And be kind to one another, tenderhearted, forgiving one another, even as God in Christ forgave you" Ephesians 4:22-32 NKJV.

"...Live in harmony with one another; be sympathetic, love as brothers, be compassionate and humble. Do not repay evil with evil or insult with insult, but with blessing, because to this you were called so that you may inherit a blessing. For, 'Whoever would love life and see good days must keep his tongue from evil and his lips from deceitful speech. He must turn from evil and do good; he must seek peace and pursue it. For the eyes of the Lord are on the righteous and his ears are attentive to their prayer, but the face of the Lord is against those who do evil.' Who is going to harm you if you are eager to do good? But even if you should suffer for what is right, you are blessed. 'Do not fear what they fear; do not be frightened.' But in your hearts set apart Christ as Lord. Always be prepared to give an answer to everyone who asks you to give the reason for the hope that you have...with gentleness and

respect, keeping a clear conscience, so that those who speak maliciously against your good behavior in Christ may be ashamed of their slander. It is better, if it is God's will, to suffer for doing good than for doing evil" 1 Peter 3:8-17 NIV.

Get Organized

"Any enterprise is built by wise planning, becomes strong through common sense, and profits wonderfully by keeping abreast of the facts. A wise man is mightier than a strong man. Wisdom is mightier than strength" Proverbs 24:3-5 TLB.

"His lord said unto him, Well done, good and faithful servant; thou hast been faithful over a few things, I will make thee ruler over many things: enter thou into the joy of thy lord" Matthew 25:23.

"Be diligent to present yourself approved to God, a worker who does not need to be ashamed, rightly dividing the word of truth" 2 Timothy 2:15 NKJV.

"Much food is in the fallow ground of the poor, And for lack of justice there is waste" Proverbs 13:23 NKJV.

8. How would you implement those lessons to affect our society and world?

9. What will you do this week to teach Kingdom principles, create models, and be organized?

PART TWO

SHIFT STUDY:

Historical Perspective: David Livingstone

David Livingstone's heart was set ablaze when he heard of the "smoke of a thousand villages where no missionary had ever been." Born into a Christian family in Scotland, he spent his youth working in a cotton mill. Although discouraged by his father, he persevered in educating himself to become one of the first Western missionaries, scientists and explorers to journey across Africa. He purposed to create a Christian commercial highway with the motto, "Christianity, Commerce and Civilization."

Livingstone experienced struggle and discouragement. At home, he was first heralded as a hero then later castigated as a failure. Barely raising enough funds to return on his final trip, he embarked to discover the source of the Nile. He promptly lost contact with the outside world until the *New York Herald* famously sent Henry Stanley to find him.

When he died in Zambia, Livingstone's heart was buried in Africa while his body was carried over a thousand miles by loyal attendants to a hero's burial in Westminster Abbey. He had named Victoria Falls and made important discoveries, but even greater, Livingstone changed the course of an entire continent as he inspired and led the way for generations of African leaders, Western abolitionists, explorers and missionaries.[1]

SHIFT PRAYER:

Father, I wish to become Your image, Your letter read by all. Use me, Father, to establish Your principles upon the place where You are planting me. I surrender my vision, energy, ambitions, and plans to You, Lord. Take them and use them for Your purposes. Father, reveal to me my sphere of influence; give me the power to take my promised land for You, Lord. In Jesus' name, Amen.

SHIFT MEDITATION:

"The steps of a good man are ordered by the Lord: and he delighteth in his way" Psalm 37:23.

I will place no value on anything I have or may possess except in relation to the kingdom of Christ.
~ David Livingstone

[1]Adapted from materials taken from www.wikipedia.org and www.ctlibrary.com

SHIFT CHALLENGE 11

PEWSHIFT

SHIFTING THE PEWS, SHIFTING THE CHURCH

Prayer Makes Everything Happen
Matthew 6:9-13

The discipline of prayer practiced by Jesus is the simplest reason why we need to start everything with prayer. Our top priority is to be like Jesus.

When we pray, something happens. When we don't pray, nothing happens. Like Jesus, before we begin any enterprise, we pray and call down the will of God to be established here in the earth as it is already established in Heaven. Prayer is about asking God to do on earth what He has already purposed in Heaven (Matt 6:9-10). Prayer is not about asking for our will to be done in heaven, in the way we have decided on earth. Prayer is the direct opposite. God is the initiator of all effective prayer. He taught us to pray for His will to be established in the earth.

At Embassy of God, the way we implement this and train new believers in prayer is through two established seasons of prayer each year. In December and July, the congregation is invited to come away to fast and pray for ten days. From one to two thousand people come throughout or for part of the fast, and pray from morning to midnight with a three-hour afternoon break. Each of our daughter churches and their worship groups lead one session. People involved in ministry bring reports so we can pray over those ministries right then. It is a powerful time with the Lord! My dream is to hold such a prayer meeting in different parts of the world, so believers everywhere can experience the thrill of prayer that we have enjoyed in Ukraine.

Laying a foundation of prayer ensures we are in tune with God. A prayer foundation provides us with strength and wisdom for the task ahead. We pray for God to use us for our heavenly purpose, to restore the earth back to God, using our God-given gifts, abilities and talents.

SHIFT YOUR THINKING:

1. Why should Jesus pray, being the Son of God? If Jesus needed to pray and fast, do we need to do the same?

2. Give instances when people pray and something happens, and when they don't and nothing happens.

3. How can you make the shift in your prayer life? In your corporate prayer? How will this help change your nation or society? Can you set aside time for intense prayer twice yearly?

Lesson Eleven

Arise from Your Prayer Closet!

PART ONE

Read the book: When to Stop Praying

Sometimes people pray without ever taking action. There is a time to leave the prayer room and carry out the plans God has revealed to you. For too many years, some Christians have concentrated only on prayer. They believe that God will supernaturally accomplish what they are asking for. But the Word of God says in James 2:17 that faith without works is useless and dead. The Kingdom does not advance on prayer alone but on prayer-inspired actions.

You will recall that when our church needed a permanent place to meet, we prayed for a year, and God was silent. That silence bothered me terribly. I couldn't understand why, when we had prayed, God hadn't done anything. I was still expecting God to do everything for us. I wasn't putting my faith into action. Finally, God had mercy on me and told me that prayer doesn't do anything by itself. "No matter how much you pray, it's not in My hands," God spoke to my heart. "The solution is in your hands. I have given you the opportunity. The people of the world don't understand prayer. They understand the language of force. Prayer is for Me, and this is not My situation. It is within your scope of influence to change it. You are on the Earth; you have the people and the power. Use your power."

SHIFT STUDY: You Will Learn

- I have prayed because I want to be with God, to get to know Him, and then to radiate His glory.
- Action without prayer is foolish.
- The revelations you receive are like foundation stones upon which you can build your life, family and calling according to God's plan.
- The Kingdom does not advance on prayer alone but on prayer-inspired actions. Countries don't develop but by prayer paired with actions.
- When you are not dead to yourself, you fear the consequences of failure.
- True humility goes where God leads, regardless of the consequences. His will is our command, no matter if it brings us life or death.
- The Kingdom belongs to doers, not hearers. One of my most important duties as a pastor is just to get people to "go"! There is a time for you to pray and a time for you to fight.

SHIFT SCRIPTURES:

Move Out

"Whatever your hand finds to do, do it with your might; for there is no work or device or knowledge or wisdom in the grave where you are going. I returned and saw under the sun that—The race is not to the swift, Nor the battle to the strong, Nor bread to the wise, Nor riches to men of understanding, Nor favor to men of skill; But time and chance happen to them all" Ecclesiastes 9:10-11 NKJV.

"And one of you says to them, 'Depart in peace, be warmed and filled,' but you do not give them the things which are needed for the body, what does it profit? Thus also faith by itself, if it does not have works, is dead. But someone will say, 'You have faith, and I have works.' Show me your faith without your works, and I will show you my faith by my works. You believe that there is one God. You do well. Even the demons believe—and tremble! But do you want to know, O foolish man, that faith without works is dead? Was not Abraham our father justified by works when he offered Isaac his son on the altar? Do you see that faith was working together with his works, and by works faith was made perfect? And

It was time for us to quit praying, and we did. Our actions led to a favorable resolution to our problem and eventually led to a change in the entire nation.

A. Not Praying!

1. When are we to stop praying? Why?

2. "Prayer is not merely a habit but a way of life." Explain ways that Christians can pray. *(page 148)*

3. Fill in the blanks: *(page 148)*

"Even youths grow _________ and ______________, and ________________ ____________ stumble and fall; but those who _______________ in the L*ORD will renew their ___________________. They will ______________ on wings like eagles; they will ___________________ and not _________________, they will _________________ and not be __________________."*

Isaiah 40:30-31

Does this familiar passage have greater meaning to you in light of this study?

B. What does God want you to do?

1. Pastor Sunday says there are two things you learn about God when you pray. Name them: *(page 149)*

   a.

   b.

2. We are building in the here-and-now what has already been established in heaven. What must we do to ensure we accomplish what He called and appointed us for? *(page 150)*

3. Name some ways we can do this.

4. If the kingdom does not advance on prayer alone, what else is required to advance the kingdom? *(page 151)*

the Scripture was fulfilled which says, 'Abraham believed God, and it was accounted to him for righteousness.' And he was called the friend of God. You see then that a man is justified by works, and not by faith only" James 2:16-24 NKJV.

"Now faith is the substance of things hoped for, the evidence of things not seen...By faith we understand that the worlds were framed by the word of God, so that the things which are seen were not made of things which are visible" Hebrews 11:1, 3 NKJV.

"The LORD our God spoke to us in Horeb, saying: 'You have dwelt long enough at this mountain. Turn and take your journey, and go to the mountains of the Amorites, to all the neighboring places in the plain, in the mountains and in the lowland, in the South and on the seacoast, to the land of the Canaanites and to Lebanon, as far as the great river, the River Euphrates'" Deuteronomy 1:6-7 NKJV.

"You have skirted this mountain long enough; turn northward" Deuteronomy 2:3 NKJV.

Change Course

"The harvest is past, The summer is ended, And we are not saved!" Jeremiah 8:20 NKJV.

"But when he came to himself, he said, 'How many of my father's hired servants have bread enough and to spare, and I perish with hunger! I will arise and go to my father, and will say to him, "Father, I have sinned against heaven and before you, and I am no longer worthy to be called your son. Make me like one of your hired servants."' And he arose and came to his father. But when he was still a great way off, his father saw him and had compassion, and ran and fell on his neck and kissed him" Luke 15:17-20 NKJV.

Act in Faith

"The Lord answered, 'If you had faith even as small as a mustard seed, you could say to this mulberry tree, "May you be uprooted and thrown into the sea," and it would obey you!'" Luke 17:6 NLT.

"Do not be anxious about anything, but in everything, by prayer and petition, with thanksgiving, present your requests to God. And the peace of God, which transcends all understanding, will guard your hearts and your minds in Christ Jesus" Philippians 4:6-7 NIV.

C. Overcoming Timidity

1. How can timidity and passivity masquerade as "humility"? *(page 152)*

2. Have you ever known anyone who seemed to pray a lot but was not very successful? In light of this study, what could be done differently?

3. In what areas is God waiting on you, when you think you are waiting on Him?

   What would you do differently now?

4. "Some countries are full of faithful believers living in poverty." How does this statement apply to your community? Your church? Your friends?

D. Become a Doer!

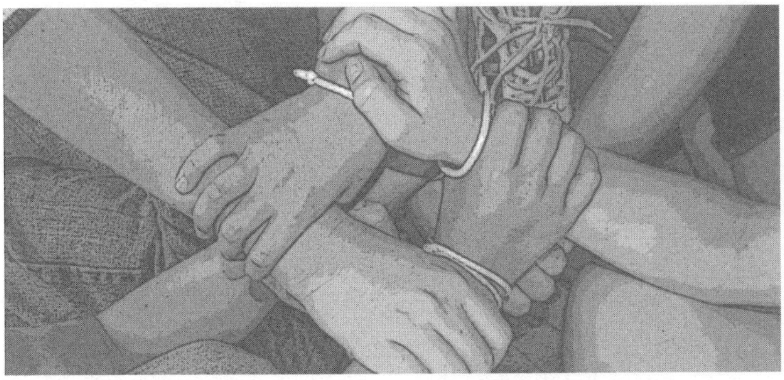

1. "The kingdom belongs to doers, not hearers. You can hear God speak all you want, but if you don't do anything, the kingdom does not rightly belong to you." *(page 153)*

   Name three things you are certain God told you to do:

   a.

   b.

   c.

2. Write a short prayer of commitment to work in each of those three areas every day this coming week:

3. Repeat this prayer each morning, then go out and DO what you know to do!

"What things soever ye desire, when ye pray, believe that ye receive them, and ye shall have them" Mark 11:24.

"And when ye stand praying, forgive, if ye have ought against any: that your Father also which is in heaven may forgive you your trespasses" Mark 11:25

"What shall we then say to these things? If God be for us, who can be against us? Nay, in all these things we are more than conquerors through him that loved us" Romans 8:31, 37.

Confidently Obey God

"When I cry unto thee, then shall mine enemies turn back: this I know; for God is for me" Psalm 56:9.

"And when they had prayed...they spake the word of God with boldness" Acts 4:31.

"But Samuel replied: 'Does the LORD delight in burnt offerings and sacrifices as much as in obeying the voice of the LORD? To obey is better than sacrifice, and to heed is better than the fat of rams'" 1 Samuel 15:22 NKJV.

"Sacrifice and offering You did not desire; My ears You have opened. Burnt offering and sin offering You did not require" Psalm 40:6 NKJV.

"Receive with meekness the engrafted word, which is able to save your souls. But be ye doers of the word, and not hearers only, deceiving your own selves" James 1:21-22 NKJV.

"In all things shewing thyself a pattern of good works..." Titus 2:7.

"Therefore, to him that knoweth to do good, and doeth it not, to him it is sin" James 4:17.

"Why do you call me Lord, Lord, and do not the things I say?" Luke 6:46.

Love People

"How God anointed Jesus of Nazareth with the Holy Ghost and with power; who went about doing good, and healing all who were oppressed of the devil; for God was with him" Acts 10:38.

"Little children, let us stop just saying we love people; let us really love them, and show it by our actions" 1 John 3:18 TLB.

"Not every one that saith unto me, Lord, Lord, shall enter into the kingdom of heaven; but he that doeth the will of my Father which is in heaven...But what think ye? A certain man had two sons; and he came to the first, and said, Son, go work to day in my vineyard. He answered and said, I will not: but afterward he repented, and went. And he came to the second, and said likewise. And he answered and said, I go,

PART TWO

SHIFT STUDY:

Historical Perspective: Billy Sunday

Fiery evangelist Billy Sunday used his professional baseball fame to draw crowds to dramatic evangelistic services that attracted top business and government leaders and influenced public policy.

Born in a poor Iowa log cabin, Sunday was sent to an orphanage after his father's Civil War death. At 15 he started work, landing in sports. While playing for Chicago, he was saved through a Gospel mission. After eight years, he left the game he loved to hold small revivals, then huge citywide crusades.

Sunday's arrival in a city eventually drew larger crowds than the President's arrival. His crusades earned more local news coverage than World War I. Presidents and politicians solicited his help. Business leaders with names like Schwab, Kresge and Rockefeller helped his crusades, some large enough to stage a 5,000-voice choir.

Sunday focused on leading people to Christ and promoted patriotism and Prohibition. He attacked preaching with fierce, uncompromising vigor, especially castigating men who abused their families. "The church needs fighting men," Sunday said, "not weasel-eyed, sponge-columned, mushy-fisted, jelly-spined, pussy-footing Christians. Lord save us from off-handed, brittle-boned, weak-kneed, thin-skinned, pliable, plastic, spineless, effeminate, three-karat Christianity."

Sunday addressed 100 million people in person and recorded 300,000 salvations.[1]

SHIFT PRAYER:

Action is the mother of production. To do nothing is to become nothing. Hence, Lord, I am praying that You will give me the ability, perseverance, and patience needed to bring Your purposes to the earth. Give me the balance of knowing when to pray and when to begin to work. Strengthen me with wisdom to know when to do what. Teach me never to lose the focus nor the balance. In Jesus' name, Amen.

SHIFT MEDITATION:

"Woe to them that are at ease in Zion..." Amos 6:1

In this Kingdom, to do nothing is to become nothing.
~ Sunday Adelaja

More men fail through lack of purpose than lack of talent.
~ Billy Sunday

[1]Adapted from materials found at www.wheaton.edu; www.wholesomewords.org; www.wikipedia.org; "The Wycliffe Biographical Dictionary of the Church," Elgin S. Moyer, 1982, ©Moody Press, Chicago, IL; *"Billy Sunday: The Man and His Message"*, by William T. Ellis, Philadelphia: John C. Winston Co., 1914; *"Billy Sunday: You've Got a Job in Detroit," by Larry D. Engelmann, Michigan History Magazine.*

sir: and went not. Whether of them twain did the will of his father? "They say unto him, The first. Jesus saith unto them, Verily I say unto you, That the publicans and the harlots go into the kingdom of God before you" Matthew 7:21; 21:28-31.

"They that sow in tears shall reap in joy" Psalm 126:5.

"A good man out of the good treasure of his heart bringeth forth that which is good...for out of the abundance of the heart his mouth speaketh" Luke 6:45.

SHIFT CHALLENGE 12

CHURCH*SHIFT*

SHIFTING THE CHURCH, *SHIFTING* THE LEADERS

The Kingdom-Driven Church
1 Timothy 3:15

At the end of a typical fairy tale, two people get married and "live happily ever after." Yet anyone married knows this is far from the end. It is only the beginning! In church, after people get saved we ask, "Are they established in a local church?" If the answer is "yes," we tend to treat this as the end of the story. But being established in a local church is not the height of our Christian faith. It is just the beginning!

Going to church is not the ultimate goal of Christian life and activity. Jesus did not ask us to sit down in church. He commissioned us to *go* from church into all the world (Matthew 28:18-20). The first Christians were not sitters, they were *goers.*

The role of the church in Scripture was not to be the end focus of the Great Commission. The focus of the Great Commission is for people who are trained in Kingdom lifestyle to "*go.*" Ensuring that new converts are established in a local church is not so we can nail them to a pew, but is for the purpose to train, release and *send* them.

People laugh when I tell them that it is my job to get rid of the members at the Embassy of God (Psalm 102:22). It sounds funny, but the truth is that on many occasions, I have had to speak privately to parishioners to tell them either to fulfill their destiny or find another church. As a result, thousands of our church members run for public office, try out in talent shows, go back to school, start non-profit organizations, seek promotions at work, pursue management training, plant other churches, become missionaries in other harvest fields or start a new business or career. As these otherwise normal church members infiltrate every sphere of society, they are collectively shaking nations.

The local church is the earthly training ground for the Kingdom. The church is not the goal or the victory, nor is it the battlefield. The church is the supplier of troops for the battlefield. The goal of the church and the believer is to subdue an ungodly world with the lifestyle of Heaven (Revelation 11:15). If we sit in the church, this will never happen.

The local church is not a place to hoard and conserve God's resources, gifts, and power. It is a headquarters for equipping and sending people. We dare not consume church resources and God's gifts for our own enjoyment when they are intended to bring God's Kingdom into the society. Salt and light are not for self consumption, but are given to save the world that God loves.

Church is not a prison. Pastors are not wardens. Members are not prisoners. Pastors do not own people. At the same time, the church cannot be owned by a board, nor its pastor owned by the members. The church is the training ground where pastors train and release people into their individual destinies (Matthew 6:33). Pastors teach so people can extend the Kingdom. People have not "achieved" the Kingdom just because they attend church and tithe. People are to take the Kingdom into their sphere of influence. People and pastors together do not sit within the four walls of a church, but bring the Kingdom to the earth and disciple nations (Matthew 6:9-10; 28:18-20).

SHIFT YOUR THINKING:

1. What is the focus of the Great Commission? How can pastors, leaders and members help each other fulfill the Great Commission?

2. In what ways can local churches hoard God's resources? In what ways can church members be encouraged to use the resources for the world?

3. If every member of a church were actively *involved* in ministry, it seems the church would eventually be empty on Sunday mornings. Instead, Embassy of God has grown. How would you account for its growth?

Lesson Twelve

Taking Steps to Victory

PART ONE

Read the book: The Orange Revolution

As a church, we had been expecting some sort of major social change for more than a year. In March 2003, I said publicly, "God is opening the heavens over Ukraine. The nation which was humiliated will start rising again. Thus says the Lord, 'Hitherto were you abased, but now by My sovereignty will I start lifting you up. I tell every humiliated one now, start moving boldly, start moving firmly, start moving bravely because your God will go in advance of you.'"

Leading up to the election, our church fasted and prayed for months for a good outcome. This tradition of relying on fasting and prayer went back to 1997 when we began holding two yearly fasts, plus monthly three-day fasts, during which we interceded for our country. The summer fast of that very year, 2004, was dedicated to the presidential elections to come. We had prepared well in prayer. During the revolution itself, four thousand of our members prayed and fasted for the potentially violent standoff to be resolved.

SHIFT STUDY: You Will Learn

- When you are obedient to God's guidance, He can literally shake the foundations of your nation.
- When the church takes a strong, visible stance in society, godly people will more easily rise to positions of influence and power.
- God may have a bigger change in mind for your sphere of influence than you currently realize.

SHIFT SCRIPTURES:

Seize Opportunities

"I returned and saw under the sun that—The race is not to the swift, Nor the battle to the strong, Nor bread to the wise, Nor riches to men of understanding, Nor favor to men of skill; But time and chance happen to them all" Ecclesiastes 9:11 NKJV.

"Now Moses was tending the flock of Jethro his father-in-law, the priest of Midian. And he led the flock to the back of the desert, and came to Horeb, the mountain of God. And the Angel of the LORD appeared to him in a flame of fire from the midst of a bush. So he looked, and behold, the bush was burning with fire, but the bush was

not consumed. Then Moses said, "I will now turn aside and see this great sight, why the bush does not burn" Exodus 3:1-3 NKJV.

"The word of God came to John the son of Zacharias in the wilderness. And he went into all the region around the Jordan, preaching a baptism of repentance for the remission of sins" Luke 3:1-3 NKJV.

"So he departed from there, and found Elisha the son of Shaphat, who was plowing with twelve yoke of oxen before him, and he was with the twelfth. Then Elijah passed by him and threw his mantle on him. And he left the oxen and ran after Elijah, and said, 'Please let me kiss my father and my mother, and then I will follow you.' And he said to him, 'Go back again, for what have I done to you?'" 1 Kings 19:19-20 NKJV.

"And he said, 'Thus says the LORD: "Make this valley full of ditches." For thus says the LORD: "You shall not see wind, nor shall you see rain; yet that valley shall be filled with water, so that you, your cattle, and your animals may drink." And this is a simple matter in the sight of the LORD; He will also deliver the Moabites into your hand'" 2 Kings 3:16-18 NKJV.

A. Foundations and Preparations

1. Go back in this study and name at least two things that Pastor Sunday and his church did to prepare for their role in a major *SHIFT* in their country:

   ____

   ____

2. Is your foundation of prayer ready to withstand a government assault, persecution, or difficulties? If not, what can you do to prepare to take your promised land?

3. "Our actions helped clear the fear from people's minds. Boldness came to everyday Ukrainians. They began to dream of freedom. They developed a willingness to fight for their rights. They saw that the government is to serve the people, not hold them captive like cattle." *(page 159)*

   Are people around you inspired to greatness and boldness?

How can a Kingdom focus in your life affect others around you?

4. In your own words, how does accepting responsibility for your community or nation affect you stepping into your personal promised land?

B. Feed the people

What happened in the streets of Kyiv may have appeared strange to some, but it was familiar to people who attended our church and other Protestant churches. There was freedom, joy, love, dancing, music, and celebration of righteousness. Nobody was violent. It was perhaps the most joyful revolution in modern times. The government was so amazed by what was happening that they accused our church of hypnotizing the country and making everyone unreasonably happy. They thought we used black magic because the mood of the protesters was just like what government spies had seen in our church. They thought we had orchestrated this massive protest, but it was the Holy Spirit who had done it. We were just trying to keep upwith His work.

But above all, people needed spiritual food during that turbulent time. The Embassy of God had published a newspaper outlining God's principles for the national transformation of Ukraine according to Kingdom principles. During the revolution, more than half a million copies were handed out to Ukrainians, fueling their hunger for spiritual awakening that went beyond political revolution.

"Then he said, 'Go, borrow vessels from everywhere, from all your neighbors—empty vessels; do not gather just a few. And when you have come in, you shall shut the door behind you and your sons; then pour it into all those vessels, and set aside the full ones.' So she went from him and shut the door behind her and her sons, who brought the vessels to her; and she poured it out. Now it came to pass, when the vessels were full, that she said to her son, 'Bring me another vessel.' And he said to her, 'There is not another vessel.' So the oil ceased... and he said, 'What can I do for you?' And Gehazi answered, 'Actually, she has no son, and her husband is old.' So he said, 'Call her.' When he had called her, she stood in the doorway. Then he said, 'About this time next year you shall embrace a son.' The woman conceived, and bore a son when the appointed time had come, of which Elisha had told her" 2 Kings 4:3-6; 10-17 NKJV.

Prepare Yourself

"And the Child grew and became strong in spirit, filled with wisdom; and the grace of God was upon Him" Luke 2:40, 52 NKJV.

"And at midnight a cry was heard: 'Behold, the bridegroom is coming; go out to meet him!' Then all those virgins arose and trimmed their lamps. And the foolish said to the wise, 'Give us some of your oil, for our lamps are going out.' But the wise answered, saying, 'No, lest there should not be enough for us and you; but go rather to those who sell, and buy for yourselves'" Matthew 25:6-9 NKJV.

"Since we have these promises...let us purify ourselves from everything that contaminates body and spirit, perfecting holiness out of reverence for God" 2 Corinthians 7:1 NIV.

Expect Victory

"And the seventy returned again with joy, saying, Lord, even the devils are subject unto us through thy name." Luke 10:18.

"Then this Daniel was preferred above the presidents and princes, because an excellent spirit was in him; and the king thought to set him over the whole realm" Daniel 6:3.

"And I say unto you, Ask, and it shall be given you; seek, and ye shall find; knock, and it shall be

1. If you could publish a newspaper for your community, what would the headlines and editorial be?

2. In your opinion, will the "chores" you are currently doing in the Lord's house get the Kingdom message to the greater community around you?

   What will you have to do to balance the housekeeping in the Lord's house with pursuing your promised land outside the church walls?

   Right now, today, are you willing to do the hard work necessary to reach this promised land?

3. Looking back at the first steps in experiencing the "shift," what outcasts of society are you willing to serve today? How could this help bring "revolution" in your community?

   Is there someone you know who is serving the outcasts with whom you could form a team?

4. How ready are you for the persecution you will face once you begin to occupy the world around you for the Kingdom?

What does this passage mean to you?
"When a man's ways are pleasing to the LORD, he makes even his enemies live at peace with him." Proverbs 16:7

5. Re-read: Suddenly the political dialogue of our country changed. Politicians were speaking in spiritual terms about the health and unity of our country and the role of God in our nation. In an interview in 2005, Yushchenko himself told the nation that "the lack of spiritual unity in Ukraine over the last ten to fourteen years is influencing every aspect of life, especially politically. I'm convinced that if we would have had more spiritual politicians, many of the things you heard about over the last months...would have been stopped by the faith of those politicians." *(page 167)*

What battles will need to be won in your community for leaders to become aware of spiritual principles?

opened unto you. For every one that asketh receiveth; and he that seeketh findeth; and to him that knocketh it shall be opened" Luke 11:9-10.

"But thou shalt remember the Lord thy God: for it is he that giveth thee power to get wealth, that he may establish his covenant which he sware unto thy fathers" Deuteronomy 8:18.

"For the Lord GOD will help me; therefore shall I not be confounded: therefore have I set my face like a flint, and I know that I shall not be ashamed" Isaiah 50:7.

"If ye abide in me, and my words abide in you, ye shall ask what ye will, and it shall be done unto you. Herein is my Father glorified, that ye bear much fruit; ... I have chosen you, and ordained you, that ye should go and bring forth fruit, and that your fruit should remain: that whatsoever ye shall ask of the Father in my name, he may give it you. John 15:7-20.

"Have I not commanded thee? Be strong and of a good courage; be not afraid, neither be thou dismayed: for the Lord thy God is with thee whithersoever thou goest. Then Joshua commanded the officers and the people" Joshua 1:9, 10.

Do It

"Let us not be weary in well doing; for in due season we shall reap, if we faint not" Galatians 6:9.

"What good is it, dear brothers and sisters, if you say you have faith but don't show it by your actions? Can that kind of faith save anyone?...Just as the body is dead without breath, so also faith is dead without good works" James 2:14-26 NLT.

"For not the hearers of the law are just before God, but the doers of the law shall be justified" Romans 2:13.

"Do not merely listen to the word, and so deceive yourselves. Do what it says. Anyone who listens to the word but does not do what it says is like a man who looks at his face in a mirror and, after looking at himself, goes away and immediately forgets what he looks like. But the man who looks intently into the perfect law that gives freedom, and continues to do this, not forgetting what he has heard, but doing it—he will be blessed in what he does" James 1:22-25 NIV.

Do you think this will be easier than it was in Ukraine? More difficult? About the same? Why?

C. **Deliverers Are Needed**

1. Who were the "Moseses" who brought deliverance to Ukraine?

2. Name some specific things they did that brought the victory of freedom to that country:

D. Bringing Freedom

1. Are people in your community ready to step into roles vacated by unbelievers who do not follow Kingdom principles?

   What must be done to prepare them?

2. What will you do this week to become even more obedient to God's guidance than you were last week?

3. God may have a bigger change in mind for your sphere of influence than you currently realize. What can you commit to, in order to be ready?

Keep At It

"Suffering produces perseverance; perseverance, character; and character, hope" Romans 5:3-5 NIV.

"So then every one of us shall give account of himself to God" Romans 14:12.

"For everyone to whom much is given, from him much will be required; and to whom much has been committed, of him they will ask the more" Luke 12:48 NKJV.

PART TWO

SHIFT STUDY:

Historical Perspective: Great Awakenings

Jonathan Edwards, a Massachusetts Congregational theologian, emphasized personal salvation, summarized in his classic sermon, "Sinners in the Hands of an Angry God." A Yale valedictorian, he studied ten more years before pastoring America's largest colonial church and sparking an intense revival in which people often fainted under the power of the Holy Spirit. The spread of the revival launched the "Great Awakening."

Oxford-educated British pastor George Whitefield was influenced by Edwards and traveled throughout the colonies, preaching several times per day with dramatic oratory skills that shook the sparsely-populated frontier. A co-founder of the Methodist movement, he became a legend on two continents.

The Great Awakening that Edwards and Whitefield started in America gave them credit as "fathers" of modern evangelicalism. The Second Great Awakening began slowly, but by 1825, the movement belonged to the persuasive New York preacher, Charles Finney. Finney won international acclaim, is credited with 500,000 conversions and is called the "father of modern revivalism."

Convinced that the gospel was meant to clean up society, Finney inspired thousands of volunteer societies organized to attack every phase of American life. Finney's work fueled the antislavery crusade, women's rights, prison reform, and temperance. He wrote, "Every member must work or quit. No honorary members."[1]

SHIFT PRAYER:

Lord, I am aware of my smallness and my limitations. Father, I pray that You will enlarge me and make me bigger than my life challenges. Prepare me, Lord; break and mend me to fit the assignment that You have for me. In Jesus' name, Amen.

SHIFT MEDITATION:

"These who have turned the world upside down have come here too" Acts 17:6 NKJV.

Resolution One: I will live for God. Resolution Two: If no one else does, I still will.
~ Jonathan Edwards

It is very remarkable, that in the book of life, we find some almost of all kinds of occupations, who notwithstanding served God in their respective generations, and shone as so many lights in the world.
~ George Whitefield

When the church finds its members falling into gross and scandalous sins, then it is time for the church to awake and cry to God for a Revival of Religion. When such things are taking place as give enemies of religion an occasion for reproach, it is time for the church to ask God, "What will become of Thy great name?" When sinners are careless and stupid, and sinking into hell unconcerned, it is time the church should bestir themselves.
~ Charles G. Finney

[1]Adapted from materials at www.ChristianityToday.com and www.wikipedia.org

SHIFT CHALLENGE 13

LEADERSHIFT

SHIFTING THE LEADERS, SHIFTING THE CHURCH

Are You a Ladder?
Matthew 20:20-28

Leaders are the ladders their people climb in order to arrive at a place of destiny and success. In my leadership position at Embassy of God, I have promised the people to be their bridge and ladder. This requires me to stay in a position that states: *I am here for you to be successful.* It requires me to have the anointing of God, the grace, and the calling to help others come to their place of destiny (Ephesians 4:11-13). As their leader, I am equipped by God to help solve people's problems and charged by God to help them find their promised land.

Some leaders manipulate others or use followers as a platform to build their own kingdom. The leader makes the people the ladders instead of being a ladder for the people. A leader may accuse active and innovative members of creating division, when the people just wanted to have their own innovative ideas heard and seen. In a church, every church member can have a vision for promoting the Kingdom of God in a unique way. Church leaders serve as ladders to help people pursue their own ministry and specific calling. Rather than focusing on the success of the leader, the focus is on the success of each member.

According to Jesus, leaders are to serve God and people. God and people are not to serve leaders. Kingdom leadership is God-focused and people-focused. Leaders pursue a place of fulfillment and lead others to a place of fulfillment as well (Mark 1:17). The leader who intentionally becomes a servant-leader is the leader who becomes truly great.

SHIFT YOUR THINKING:

1. Who has served as a "ladder" or a "bridge" for you in your life, to help you get from one place in life to another? To whom could you become a ladder, to help them achieve what God has placed in their hearts to do?

2. How can leaders and members help each other fulfill their various visions and callings without rebellion or division?

3. What can you do today to become someone's ladder?

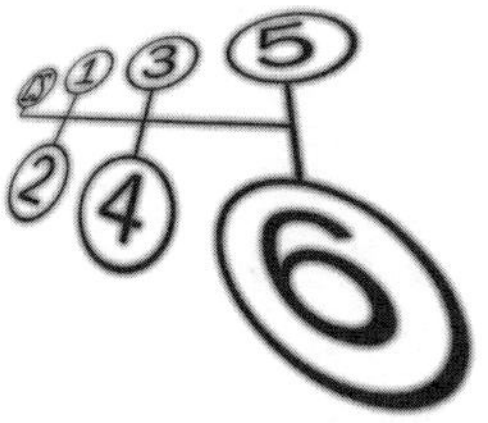

Lesson Thirteen

Celebrate Your Personal Grand Opening

PART ONE

Read the book: The World Is Waiting for You

Whether or not you realize it, you are a wanted person. The world is waiting for you to find your promised land and deliver people from the kingdom of darkness. We all have our own promised lands, commissioned to us from God—those special areas in society that desperately need our help. The world is waiting for the rulers of those promised lands to appear—you and me. Lost people want God's polished arrows to strike at the heart of injustice and unrighteousness. People know they need solutions to their problems and crises. They need to be unshackled. The Bible says:

For the earnest expectation of the creation eagerly waits for the revealing of the sons of God. For the creation was subjected to futility, not willingly, but because of Him who subjected it in hope; because the creation itself also will be delivered from the bondage of corruption into the glorious liberty of the children of God. For we know that the whole creation groans and labors with birth pangs together until now. Romans 8:19-22 NKJV

God has allowed the world to be subjected to futility so that we might set people free with news of His Kingdom. We have all the answers. We are indispensable to the health and well-being of our nations. The world simply cannot do without us.

SHIFT STUDY: You Will Learn

- The Christian community is largely mute on the major issues of the day. The world is waiting for you to find your promised land and deliver people from the kingdom of darkness.
- Lost people want God's polished arrows to strike at the heart of injustice and unrighteousness. We are indispensable to the health and well-being of our nations.
- Everyone living without God is in torment.
- Until you arrive in your promised land, people will grope around looking for solutions in the wrong places.
- The government can pass bills, but only the Great Healer can mend a broken soul.
- When you give your life for the gospel's sake, you often get back a much better life.
- God wants to use us so that His glory might fill the earth. It is His glory we carry, not our own.

SHIFT **SCRIPTURES:**

Deliver People

"Rescue those who are unjustly sentenced to die; save them as they stagger to their death. Don't excuse yourself by saying, "Look, we didn't know." For God understands all hearts, and he sees you. He who guards your soul knows you knew. He will repay all people as their actions deserve" Proverbs 24:11-12 NLT.

"God gave us the 'ministry of reconciliation' and committed to us the 'message of reconciliation'" 2 Corinthians 5:16-21 NIV.

"Blessed are the merciful: for they shall obtain mercy. Blessed are the pure in heart: for they shall see God. Blessed are the peacemakers: for they shall be called the children of God" Matthew 5:7-9.

"For God hath not given us the spirit of fear; but of power, and of love, and of a sound mind" 2 Timothy 1:7.

"Thy word is a lamp unto my feet, and a light unto my path. I have sworn, and I will perform it, that I will keep thy righteous judgments. I am afflicted very much: quicken me, O LORD, according unto thy word. Accept...the freewill offerings of my mouth, O LORD, and teach me thy judgments. My soul is continually in my hand: yet do I not forget thy law. The

A. "The Christian Community Is Largely Mute"

1. What can Christians do to help solve the world's greatest needs and major issues of the day? *(page 177)*

2. Why do non-Christians carry God's burden for the poor, the unhealthy, the prisoner, the orphan, the downtrodden and many Christians do not? *(page 178)*

3. What Christian do you know who has been on the leading edge of solving one of the world's great problems?

B. People in the World Are Suffering!

1. Do you believe that everyone without Christ suffers from futility and lives in some form of torment? *(page 179)*

   Was there a day when you were like that? Can you recall how it felt?

2. "All people have an inner emptiness that drives them to seek Him. That's why there is so much idol worship in many nations. In a vacuum, people look for something to worship. Some nations worship money, sex, power, sports, and so on." *(pages 179-180)*

   Name specific people who likely depend on you to show them how to live by Kingdom principles.

   a.

   b.

   c.

   d.

   e.

   f.

   g.

3. What part of your life is hardest for you to give up for the Lord?

   Circle the following activities that would be difficult for you to forego in order to pursue your promised land and help needy people.

   Surfing the Internet
   Sleeping late
   Gardening
   Playing or watching sports
   Going out with friends
   Working
   Watching television
   Shopping
   Cooking or eating
   Working on your house or car
   Taking your children to various lessons and activities
   Reading the newspaper

wicked have laid a snare for me: yet I erred not from thy precepts. Thy testimonies have I taken as an heritage for ever: for they are the rejoicing of my heart. I have inclined mine heart to perform thy statutes alway, even unto the end" Psalm 119:105-112.

Give Fearlessly

"It is possible to give away and become richer! It is also possible to hold on too tightly and lose everything. Yes, the liberal man shall be rich! By watering others, he waters himself... Trust in God and flourish as a tree!" Proverbs 11:24, 28 TLB.

"My little children, let us not love in word, neither in tongue; but in deed and in truth" 1 John 3:18.

"There is no fear in love; but perfect love casteth out fear: because fear has torment" 1 John 4:18.

"And when they were come to him, he said unto them, Ye know, from the first day that I came into Asia, after what manner I have been with you at all seasons, Serving the LORD with all humility of mind, and with many tears, and temptations, which befell me by the lying in wait of the Jews: And how I kept back nothing that was profitable unto you, but have shewed you, and have taught you publicly, and from house to house, Wherefore I take you to re-

cord this day, that I am pure from the blood of all men. For I have not shunned to declare unto you all the counsel of God. Take heed therefore unto yourselves, and to all the flock, over the which the Holy Ghost hath made you overseers, to feed the church of God, which he hath purchased with his own blood" Acts 20:18-28.

"But do not forget to do good and to share, for with such sacrifices God is well pleased" Hebrews 13:16 NKJV.

"For who has known or understood the mind (the counsels and purposes) of the Lord so as to guide and instruct Him and give Him knowledge? But we have the mind of Christ (the Messiah) and do hold the thoughts (feelings and purposes) of His heart" 1 Corinthians 2:16 AMP.

"His lord said unto him, Well done, good and faithful servant; thou hast been faithful over a few things, I will make thee ruler over many things: enter thou into the joy of thy lord" Matthew 25:23.

Start Now!

"Even when I am old and gray, do not forsake me, O God, till I declare your power to the next generation, your might to all who are to come" Psalm 71:18 NIV

"For our gospel did not come to you in word only, but also in power, and in

C. Did the Donkey Take a Bath?

Jesus needed a donkey to enter Jerusalem. He needs the same thing to enter your areas of influence. God is saying to us today: "I want to enter your city. I want to enter your school. I want to come into your workplace and your social sphere. I want to be with your family. The harvest is great, and I need laborers and co-workers. I am ready to impact your areas of influence through you. But I need your help. I need someone to carry My influence there."

Anything I have attained in Ukraine or elsewhere is because I have made myself a donkey for Christ. When Jesus entered the city, people welcomed Him with enthusiasm, strewing the road with their garments and with branches from the trees. But I'm sure they barely noticed the animal He rode in on. Yes, this creature had an important mission, to carry the Master. But his mission was about Jesus, not about his own reputation as a worthy pack animal. Carrying the Son of God was enough for him.

1. Many Christians feel they need seminary or elaborate preparations in order to be used by God. In the story of the donkey, did the donkey smell good? Did the disciples bathe the donkey before Jesus used it? How does this apply to your life? *(page 182)*

2. Must we be perfect before we can be used by God?

3. People do not need YOU personally as much as they need the God that you carry. What does this mean to you as you step into your promised land?

D. Have a Grand Opening!

Imagine your life is a big empty store, having a grand opening as a "Kingdom Principles Mart."

1. What need(s) in the community will your store meet?

   How would you communicate Kingdom principles through your store?

2. What do you still need to learn about operating your store before it can open?

3. If you are called to a social area to meet some social needs, how would you begin? What steps do you need to take to bring Kingdom influence through your calling?

the Holy Spirit and in much assurance, as you know what kind of men we were among you for your sake. And you became followers of us and of the Lord, having received the word in much affliction, with joy of the Holy Spirit, so that you became examples to all in Macedonia and Achaia who believe" 1 Thessalonians 1:5-7 NKJV.

"My message and my preaching were not with wise and persuasive words, but with a demonstration of the Spirit's power" 1 Corinthians 2:4.

"Ye are the light of the world. A city that is set on an hill cannot be hid. Neither do men light a candle, and put it under a bushel, but on a candlestick; and it giveth light unto all that are in the house. Let your light so shine before men, that they may see your good works, and glorify your Father which is in heaven" Matthew 5:14-16.

Pure Heart

"Yet I will rejoice in the LORD, I will joy in the God of my salvation" Habakkuk 3:18.

"All scripture is given by inspiration of God, and is profitable...That the man of God may be perfect, thoroughly furnished unto all good works" 2 Timothy 3:16, 17

"After removing Saul, he made David their king. He testified concerning him: 'I have found David son of

Jesse a man after my own heart; he will do everything I want him to do'" Acts 13:22 NIV.

"All a man's ways seem innocent to him, but motives are weighed by the LORD...All a man's ways seem right to him, but the LORD weighs the heart" Proverbs 16:2; 21:2 NIV.

"Create in me a clean heart, O God; and renew a right spirit within me. Cast me not away from thy presence; and take not thy holy spirit from me. Restore unto me the joy of thy salvation; and uphold me with thy free spirit. Then will I teach transgressors thy ways; and sinners shall be converted unto thee" Psalm 51:10-13.

"The righteous shall move onward and forward; those with pure hearts shall become stronger and stronger" Job 17:9 TLB.

"Delight thyself also in the Lord; and he shall give thee the desires of thine heart. Commit thy way unto the Lord; trust also in him; and he shall bring it to pass" Psalm 37:4-5.

Jesus said, *"Greater love hath no man than this, that a man lay down his life for his friends"* John 15:13.

4. If your call is to politics, how can politics serve the purposes of God? How would you do this?

5. How would you bring God to media if that is your ministry calling?

6. Do you know some people who are called to change the sphere of sports or education with God's values? How do you think this could be accomplished?

7. What is the purpose of business and finances? If God called you to the business world, how would you establish the Kingdom upon this sphere of life?

8. What do you expect to happen to people in your community through the service of your ministry?

9. How can a culture be changed through your efforts and ministry? What effect would this have on you?

10. What day is your Grand Opening?

"What is our hope, our joy, or the crown in which we will glory in the presence of our Lord Jesus when he comes? Is it not you? Indeed, you are our glory and joy" 1 Thessalonians 2:18-20 NKJV.

"On that day they will say to Jerusalem, 'Do not fear, O Zion; do not let your hands hang limp. The LORD your God is with you, he is mighty to save. He will take great delight in you, he will quiet you with his love, he will rejoice over you with singing.'" Zephaniah 3:16-18.

PART TWO

SHIFT STUDY:

Current Perspective: The Ukrainian Revolutionaries Who *SHIFTED*

GOVERNMENT*SHIFT*

Oleksandr Malomedov, a former drug addict, launched a successful church, then launched a government-funded training program for social and government workers. He has now trained and planted over 200 people in various government institutions for the purpose of influencing decisions for the Kingdom.

ART*SHIFT*

Vadym Laznyevyy became the top deejay in Ukraine to redeem the entertainment world for the Lord. With his fame, he influences people for the Kingdom and with his funds, he helps Kingdom initiatives launched by others.

Sergiy Rozvadovskiy, a former casino owner, determined to influence the arts. His first film, "One for All," was fast-paced and funny, yet illustrated the principles of Jesus giving His life for all. It became 2005's most popular youth film and attracted a fan club of twelve million people.

SOCIAL*SHIFT*

Iurii Salii was captured as the "godfather" of the Kyivskiy mafia family. In prison, he met Christ and, through Embassy of God's prison programs, became a prison pastor. Now free, he trains more pastors for prisons than other agencies do for churches. His prison pastors number over 1000.

Anatoliy Bilonozhko is the Bishop of the Embassy of God (Pastor Sunday is the Senior Pastor). A former alcoholic, he now oversees 650 churches, with a goal of planting 1000 more. Every month, his teams plant 10 new churches.

Nataliya Potopaeva, one of the first church members and a former alcoholic, built a congregation of 3000 people in Kiev and founded a rehabilitation center that has graduated 5000. She planted 30 churches in Ukraine with pastors trained during rehabilitation. She is now a missionary to Germany.

EDUCATION*SHIFT*

Tetiana Galushko was chased out of school as a teen and became a drug addict and prostitute. After salvation, Tetiana determined to help high school students. She wrote morality curriculum with Kingdom principles that is now used by over 100,000 students and is being adopted by the Ministry of Education.

Oleksandr Korman worked his way onto national television and declared, "I am a virgin and I'm not ashamed of it." He started an institute to teach young men and women to be responsible spouses and parents, which was adopted as a national program. The government now pays his staff, all church members, and he provides the materials.

BUSINESS*SHIFT*

Glib Spivakov, a former casino owner, started health centers where people receive free treatments and hear wellness messages that preach Kingdom principles. Paying members receive side benefits and finance the centers. In two years Glib has ministered through his business to over three million people face-to-face. He now has 250 centers in over 20 countries.

MEDIA*SHIFT*

Liliya Roman is the reigning Miss Ukraine. Attending church since age 8, she realized God gave her beauty as a tool. Entering the contest at the last minute, she won and became a mass media spokesperson for Kingdom principles.

SHIFT PRAYER:

I believe Your Word, Lord, that the whole world is waiting for me. I now realize that I need not become perfect before I can be used of God. So, Lord, I pray You begin to direct and use me even now from where I am. Help me, Lord, to be faithful in little so that You can trust me with much more. In Jesus' name, Amen.

SHIFT MEDITATION:

"I can do all things through Christ who strengthens me" Philippians 4:13 NKJV.